A YEAR OF DAYS

A YEAR OF DAYS

Beatrice Nash Horowitz

iUniverse, Inc.
New York Lincoln Shanghai

A YEAR OF DAYS

iUniverse books may be ordered through booksellers or by contacting:

iUniverse
2021 Pine Lake Road, Suite 100
Lincoln, NE 68512
www.iuniverse.com
1-800-Authors (1-800-288-4677)

Photography
Mark Horowitz
Beatrice Horowitz

ISBN-13: 978-0-595-40699-9 (pbk)
ISBN-13: 978-0-595-85063-1 (ebk)
ISBN-10: 0-595-40699-8 (pbk)
ISBN-10: 0-595-85063-4 (ebk)

Printed in the United States of America

For M(ark)

Without him none of this would have happened

Contents

1

Beginnings

The tractor truck roared past on our left, flashing us a glimpse of a stylized death's head on its passenger door before the dusty trailer inched by, daring us to reach out and touch its spiny sides. Just beyond our front bumper, the monstrosity rocked to its right and cleared us by a foot, sending shuddering wind currents back over our rig. The passing shadow gave way to blinding late afternoon sunlight that cut through our own cab and slid around the edges of our sunglasses. Mark hunched over the steering wheel, profile grimly set, and for a few seconds his swearing actually halted. Sweat trickled down my neck, and misery locked my jaw and stung my eyes. The dog pressed harder up against my chest and sobbed. We were off on our dream trip.

Dawn had come early and hot on the day that my husband and I left our condo in Brookline and headed onto the road for a year of traveling. I was already alert by the time the bedroom windows faded from glittery black to sullen gray. Mark's immobile body and steady breathing next to me betrayed his own wakefulness. As a perpetual insomniac, he claims not to have slept since 1964. When he does sleep, he thrashes about, gasping and muttering, and occasionally stops breathing altogether. Myself, I require and regularly get my eight hours of thoughtless restfulness each night. Which meant that my foreshortened sleep this morning would guarantee a ragged mental fragility for the rest of the day. This peeved me slightly. I stared at the ceiling and tried to will myself back to sleep. Mark rolled over towards my profile. "Might as well get up." I dressed and started coffee with no idea that the lack of eight hours' rest would seem comically trivial once I hit the road to wander around North America in an RV for twelve months.

By six-thirty we'd transferred the last of the cartons from our third floor condo to the car on the street, anxiously accompanied up and down every stair climb by our little spaniel-poodle mix. The apartment had been stripped of everything personal and valuable, to await the arrival of the three new Boston College grads who had rented it for the year. There was no use starting out so early. The dealer where our RV waited for us would not even open until nine o'clock. The weight and warmth of the coffee mug between my hands anchored me in a small comfort zone laced with hot caffeine. The sun had hit the tops of the living room windows. Outside, the front bay windows of the houses across the way curved their four-tiered, hundred-year-old facades gently down the bend of our block, rhythmically descending the hill towards boisterous Beacon Street. Soft red brick beat a syncopated three-quarter rhythm, marked off by gray cement cornices into the individual house measures of windows and door moldings. Above the modest curves of roof ledges, a transparent blue sky gathered intensity. The rising sun moved down through our windows to pick out parallelograms on the floor, highlighting polished wood and the corner of an orange and green rug pattern.

I loved this place. I was leaving this place. Did this make any sense at all? Tomorrow morning I would awaken and make coffee in an RV whose square footage of living space could fit easily inside our dining room. My dream home had become a mere commodity for providing income to pay our bills while we traveled. My logical brain had made this decision and did not regret it. My emotional brain screamed out, "This is my home! This is mine! Mine! All others keep out!" Standing there in the kitchen, heat starting to gather in the room's corners and waver in the sunlight, I touched the side of my head where it throbbed slightly with lack of sleep. The coffee cooled in my mug. Mark appeared at the kitchen entrance.

"Let's go." He banged his cup on the counter. Murray, the dog, jumped to attention beside the front door, then followed my wobbly legs down to the street. An hour south on Route One our brand new vehicle home sat dripping wires from its internal panels into the rocky dirt of the dealer's back lot. Tom, the garrulous owner, unlocked the chain link fence and informed us that Mike, the service manager and the core of all useful activity at this business, had not yet arrived. Half an hour crept by before Mike appeared, charming and congratulatory, and disappeared elsewhere. We waited some more. A man known as Ray, the electronics whiz, called to Mark, and the two of them climbed into the vehicle and began pulling free whatever wires weren't already dangling, so that they could exclaim over them. Seems the twelve-volt system didn't work, whatever that was. I didn't care, but the men appeared to care a lot.

We'd originally planned to buy a used camper and had been surprised to be able to afford a new model. On a new model, everything would be clean, everything would work. It'd be like driving a new car off the lot. Maybe a lever would be stiff or something, but the absolute reliability of brand new could be counted on.

Not so. Not so at all. First there had been the wait. The camper was being built to "our specifications," somewhere in Alabama. "Our specifications" sounded wonderful, as if a team of skilled artisans was carefully fitting the pieces together with constant reference to the written order sent to them from our dealer. "Our specifications" really meant that it took almost two months for the thing to roll off the assembly line, during which time we were asked every couple of weeks to fork over another few thousand dollars. Were we being complete suckers? Spring had gone from rain to mud to green, every other arrangement to go wandering for a year had been made, and yet we had waited.

Now I was spending our departure day still writhing in anticipation, walking Murray in the brush at the back of the dealer's lot, getting fast food for lunch, and listening to the car radio. The afternoon heat reached full intensity and began to fade. Then the last panel clicked back into place over its miasma of wires, and Mark drove the huge clanking thing slowly forward to where we could hook the car onto the back.

"Hold up, you don't have your welcoming packet yet," Mike called. Fifteen minutes of searching yielded this vital item: a cardboard box filled with a broom and dust pan, four rolls of toilet paper, packets of septic deodorizer, and a note-pad with the dealer's phone number printed on each sheet. The whole process of the day was beginning to feel like wrenching a baby from a reluctant birthing unit. These people sold the traveling machines, but they resisted launching them from the nest.

Suddenly Tom's small, practical partner and wife, Janet, stepped forward. "Take me with you." The truth of her envy shone through her joke. Tom hugged me. How funny, I thought. These people that we hardly know provide our official farewell. They lined up to watch as we climbed into the cab and fastened our seatbelts. Mark went through five minutes of adjustment, flipping switches and fiddling with mirrors while he muttered to himself, and then turned on the engine. The whole machine crept forward towards the open gate. Murray jumped off the couch and sat on the floor next to me, whimpering.

In front of us the traffic of Route One swept past in a deluge of SUVs, pick-ups, and the occasional sports model. M began a steady stream of soft swearing back over his left shoulder. Finally a lagging sedan offered a precarious opening, and he tromped on the accelerator and trundled us out onto the pavement. The camper rocked ponderously, the engine roared steadily, and the driver kept up his chant of obscenities. He's just talking to himself, I thought, that's okay. I kept trying to regulate my breathing through my mouth while I stroked Murray's head. We lumbered along Route One with tiny vehicles buzzing angrily around us. The nacreous green Interstate signs loomed, and we curved right to climb the ramp. At the top of the slope three lanes of traffic whizzed past. A tractor-trailer boomed along in the right lane, blowing us slightly sideways back into the entry lane. "I can't do this. I can't do this," Mark started yelling. At the same time he twisted the wheel, and our nose moved out into the traffic, all the weight of our rig swaying in the wind fanning off the truck in front of us. Murray took one leap and landed in my lap, where he began crying out loud. I gave up all attempts at regular breathing and took up a ragged panting.

Next to my right foot a small rectangular window inserted into the side of the vehicle afforded me a view of the white line whipping by us at the outer edge of the highway. Perhaps this window was the manufacturer's deliberate attempt to terrorize me. If so, the attempt succeeded. From time to time the line disappeared from view as we rocketed along. I would wait breathlessly for about three seconds for it to reappear, and then I'd shriek at Mark, "The white line! The white line!" He replied incoherently, but I got the intended message: shut up.

There was only one way to control my panic and comply with his request. I closed my eyes. Okay, if the whole rig was going to tip sideways into the grassy slope at the highway's edge, crushing me first as it rolled over, what was the point of seeing it coming? You might think it would be hard to tear myself away from the sight of all this. It quickly became the most seductive of options.

By the time we'd been on the road for two hours, I was convinced that I might never breathe normally again. Bouncing along watching the traffic zoom ahead of us, jouncing sideways when the semi-tractors passed us, listening to M's muttered swearing, trying to keep my eyes off that blur of white line by my foot, I gasped for air like a grounded guppy. But if I just closed my eyes, my heart would slow, and my breath would steady. Maybe I could spend the whole year with my eyes closed. This began to seem like a very appealing idea.

"We need gas." Mark's lucid statement broke through his unintelligible profanities and forced my eyes open. Gas! God, we had just made it past the fury of Boston beltway commuter traffic and gained a little space around us in southern New Hampshire. Couldn't we keep rolling on this way indefinitely? No, of course not. This internal combustion engine had the same demands of every other such engine on the planet. We chose an off-ramp with a sign promising three different brands of gas and teetered off the highway. While I was still examining our choices and considering what to suggest, Mark swerved left into the first station. Half a dozen cars screeched to a halt in front of our right flank as we slowly made an enormous arc and inched forward towards the outside pump. We made it in one try, which was a good thing. Miss by an inch, and we would need to unhook the car and start again, as backing the full rig up wasn't an option. Later in our trip we did sometimes miss the gas pumps and leapt out to struggle with the tow bar, while amused customers watched us from the corners of their eyes. But on our first day we were spared this humiliation. We refueled without knocking over the pumps or taking a header into the station's canopy with our roof. Back on the road the White Mountains reared up around an emptying highway. A tremendous sense of accomplishment seemed to overtake M, and he stopped swearing and laughed out loud. For myself, I went on closing my eyes whenever I felt like it.

Moving In

2

No Perfect Life

When I did open my eyes they filled with the bright light of a June evening decorating southern New Hampshire. We were headed for my mother's home in northern Vermont, to attend my older brother's sixtieth birthday and drop off the dog for the year. Murray's steady sobbing in my lap confirmed our decision to leave him there. At eight years old, he'd be happier in a stationary home, a good companion for my elderly mother. We didn't ask his opinion. That's the advantage of dogs over children: they can't contradict you when you decide you know what's best for them.

Flocks of crows and sparrows tumbled above us, pursuing their last feeding search of the day. Hawks conducted their own solitary hunts in floating passes across the highway. If one of those hawks had possessed x-ray vision, he could have looked down at the inside of a small home rattling along the ribbon of pavement, thirty-one feet long and slightly over eight feet wide, two people sitting at the front end of it staring out the windshield, one of them clutching the steering wheel and the other with her arms wrapped around a trembling dog. If the hawk had cared, he could have observed the layout of living space that this small family considered essential. Directly behind the driving area, a dinette booth lined the left wall and a couch bordered the right wall, separated by a narrow strip of carpet. The home's mid-section, near the entry door, was given over to a kitchen outfitted with a refrigerator, a sink, a stove and a tiny square of work counter. From here an even narrower passageway split the counter holding a bathroom sink from the cubicle that enclosed the toilet and shower. In the last section, a wide bed obliterated the remaining floor space. Finally, behind the rear wall of all this, the empty car sashayed along on its hitch.

To the hawk drifting by on an updraft, in search of a simple dinner and a secure branch for the night, this must have seemed an inexplicably cumbersome way to travel. Indeed, our first weeks on the road were marked by twinned struggles with the huge clumsiness of the outside of our rig and the constricted awkwardness of the inside. I couldn't do anything without closely choreographing my actions to M's movements. If he stood brushing his teeth at the bathroom sink, I was either trapped in the bedroom or denied access to that space. Since when, I wondered, had he been so dedicated to dental hygiene? Dressing to go out had to be done in shifts, as only one person at a time could access the closet. M would plant himself in front of this cabinet for several minutes, contemplating his collection of four sweaters, while I stared at his back and marveled at the care he now put into dressing himself. Had he always been this fashion conscious? I certainly hadn't noticed it when we each enjoyed our own closet.

We exchanged a lot of, "I'm sorry." "No, I'm sorry," in the beginning. There were flashes of irritation on both sides, a quick, sharp phrase, followed by an apology within an hour or so. It was our dance of accommodation, and we kept it up for weeks, up through Granby and Montreal in Quebec, back down to Cape Cod, and west through Massachusetts into upper New York State. It took that long and that many miles to work our way up to a blow out fight.

In twenty-seven years, we'd done our share of battling. Like a pair of boxers without a referee, we'd done enough close-in fighting to learn each other's moves and develop our countermoves. Our worst combat left us binding our wounds; our best disputes led to greater understanding. Two people struggling for intimacy beyond the walls of gender differences and adult remnants of differing childhood lessons will, if they are lucky, grow both tenderer and more resilient with each other in the heat of their friction. In our years together, Mark and I had done some damage and we'd made some gains, but neither one of us ever shrank from the war. My husband's background and disposition had convinced him that a direct attack was his best response to my sometimes convoluted maneuvers to explain and improve our relationship. In turn, I'd jump into the brawl with all the verbal skills I'd gained growing up with three brothers. We fought about how to raise our sons, we fought about how to spend money, and we fought about what exceeded acceptable flirting in social situations. In recent years, with the children grown, the money secure, and the sexual byplay in friendships waning, our battles had subsided and almost disappeared. I might not be absolutely sure of his daily moods, but by now I never doubted his rock solid presence. So what exactly was this semi-polite, exquisitely careful verbal fox trot that we were doing? Out on the road, with no job to escape to each day, limited opportunities for long solitary walks, not even a solid door to slam on each other, we were just plain afraid to engage. Like armies without retreat options, we shared an uneasiness about committing to combat without a secure exit strategy.

The last two months in Brookline, after we'd left our jobs, we'd already negotiated signal systems for sharing each other's constant company. In our familiar surroundings we experimented with ways to indicate that one wanted some time alone, with how to introduce a topic that needed joint decision-making, or how to suggest a course of action without implying a definite opinion. We weren't using the word "retired" about our latest routines, but we congratulated each other on how skilled we appeared to be at these transactions, "for the future, when it's full time, you know?" Nervousness bounced around in our days, but our confidence in our abilities was high. We were about to go off on an adventure together. Confessing our jitters to each other only strengthened our mutual conviction that we would solve all obstacles together.

The day we sailed out onto the road, my emotional life cast off all lines to its well-worn moorings and drifted out onto unknown currents. When I was very small, before grade school, a recurring dream visited me in which I would wade into the ocean and feel the water rising, past my knees, up over my hips to reach to my waist and then lap at my chest. I'd begin to splash at the rising tide, trying to push it away, then I'd jerk awake, panting with terror. When I started school and began mastering my lessons, the dream disappeared. For the last fifty years I had grown confident of my abilities to swim in life's currents or drop my feet and plant my tread, keeping my head above water. Sailing along in the camper, the water was rising on me again, obscuring the sense of a solid bottom. The preschool dream revisited my sleep. I wasn't exactly drowning, but I didn't know how long my frantic movements with legs and arms would keep me afloat. Awake, I kept up my paddling, hoping for calm seas and avoiding the risk of capsizing in a stormy encounter with M. I moved from one challenge to another in trying to learn our new life style, too tired to contemplate why my sense of competency had completely evaporated.

Our new vehicle simultaneously freed us to wander about the geography and imprisoned us with its space and demands. Every new campsite required gingerly maneuverings, with M backing and forwarding, and me outside in the dirt, rushing side-to-side and yelling directions. Once in place, M tackled the lines for water, electric, and sewer connections. I went inside to arrange lamps, kitchen equipment, pictures and plants; whatever might make our stay in this site feel like home, even temporarily.

Early in the trip, I proposed to M that the tradeoff for his sewer work would be that I would do all the inside work, and he accepted. The bathroom was miniscule: the shower trickled against my shoulder blades, the toilet system needed regular attention, and the tiny, low sink splashed water against my groin.

The bed had to be made by sidling around it and stuffing the coverings between knees and mattress as best as possible. But the kitchen was the worst of it. Imagine cooking in a dollhouse that some kind grandfather has rigged out with working plumbing and gas. Mindful of the refrigerator's ability to lose all its chill in a flash, I would open the door, snatch everything that I needed to prepare supper and pile it on the three square feet of counter space. From here things spontaneously flung themselves onto the floor. I'd gather the errant items up and place them on the table, from where they would tumble to the dinette bench.

Food and its preparation comfort me greatly in times of stress. I can't tell whether the fixing or the eating is more important. Feeling disoriented? Ground yourself with a good meal, assembled with care. Combine the comfort foods of yourself and your companions. Come away soothed and stronger. Even in our tent camping days, when our sons were small, I'd balance a big fry pan on the green propane stove and cook bacon and eggs, grilled sandwiches, and steak dinners. The campers next door would share a can of cold baked beans and duck back inside their tent, while I stood in the dirt and fought off insects and rain in order to serve the family hot meals. So this RV kitchen's tile floor, running hot water, three burner stove, and combination microwave/convection oven should have been luxurious fun to use. The model on the sales floor had promised breezy cooking sessions. The reality out on the road was anything but.

You can't cook if you can't chop and stir. You can't chop and stir without some kind of horizontal surface. I had to stop covering the counter with ingredients and leaving myself no workspace. Simple, you say. It sounds simple in the recounting, but in the first weeks on the road, with my mind disobediently off center, such transparent dictums tended to escape me.

There is a side of me that my parents used to call stubborn. When confronted with difficulty, I have a tendency to dig my heels in, lower my thick head and use my skull to batter on the object of my frustration. Suggestions to try another way only serve to convince me that others lack my ability to eventually overcome this barrier and break through in triumph. So I continued my approach for a while, chopping, dropping, and swearing. Once the ingredients were prepared, pans went onto the stove. It quickly became apparent that the presence of three burners was just decorative. Only two burners could be used at any one time.

The stove was not as frustrating as the sink. Wedged into the corner was a double sink, one side just big enough to hold two highball glasses, the other side marginally bigger, with a toy strainer at the bottom, sized for a child's fingers. I was sure I'd gotten the better end of the deal when M took over the sewer and left me the inside jobs. But after dinner, contemplating a sink full of rapidly cooling, greasy water, with that tiny strainer bobbing around on the surface, rising screams thickened my throat.

I didn't actually scream, I just muttered. The two of us seemed to be developing a sort of gritted-teeth style, in which it was forbidden to let loose to any genuine degree with frustration or anger. In between these clench-jawed moments we were still elated by our actions, exclaiming daily over our freedom and our new surroundings. There were moments of giddy laughter and lots of handholding. We had sex three times as often as we'd had at home. In spite of the confines of the kitchen, I cooked a lot, and we ate with relish. We drank quite a lot, making happy toasts to each other every night. Almost every day we got out our bikes and enjoyed the warmth of muscles working hard. I read and drew; I played the keyboard.

Then without warning, euphoria would collapse into despair. An unreturned phone call from one of our sons, or the sight of a family group wandering through the campground, and I'd plunge into black hopelessness. This could also happen with no evident cause, right in the middle of savoring a terrific novel. Life would seem meaningless, and the remnant of it left to me too short and useless. I did not tell these feelings to M, any more than I expressed the alarming rage I felt when he spoke shortly, did not follow my directions, or failed to express appreciation for my struggles in the kitchen. Any admission of a state of mind less than joyful might capsize my emotional boat.

So we skittered along through the first weeks, keeping up appearances, cracking our elbows on the corners of our tiny home, and silently fighting off the fear of the empty spaces opening in our hearts. At times I felt physically dizzy. M said he felt disoriented. We both missed Murray. Missing the dog was the one sadness that it was safe for us to talk about. Except for occasional irritable outbursts, quickly smoothed with an apology, we maintained our mutual silence about all other things negative. We seemed to have struck an unspoken understanding that direct confrontation was to be avoided as long as possible. Such confrontation might prove too dangerous in this tiny, shared space, surrounded by strange terrain. Once we started, we might destroy our determined belief that we were on a dream trip, and then what?

A heat wave gripped North America that summer, withering plant and animal life, depleting water reservoirs, and destroying crops. People died in Chicago. Radio stations broadcast news of broken high temperature records and advisories to stay indoors and drink lots of fluids. We slept with the air conditioner running. The second week in July we were headed west on the New York State Thruway. The pavement undulated out in front of us under the distortion of the torrid air, bordered by wilting deciduous woods. In the shimmering distance, some dark objects appeared on the highway. We rumbled towards them, squinting, M muttering, "What the hell?" The objects got bigger and reeled about in the rising heat waves as we bore down on them.

We yelled together, "They're geese! They're geese!" A flock of a dozen birds was attempting to walk across the Thruway, no doubt disoriented by the fiery weather. In a car, we would have swerved around the hapless beasts. An RV with an auto in tow does not swerve or do anything else quickly (unless, of course, I was right about its propensity to tip over.). And it doesn't stop on a dime. We bore down on these birds, which seemed to have forgotten that they could fly. M laid on the horn, and we both started yelling, "Move! Move!" Just in time, the leader turned and herded his followers in an awkward lumber back to the highway shoulder. We swept by, our bodies still tensed for impact.

Two minutes later M started to laugh. He rubbed his hands alternately on his pants legs to dry their sweat and squinted at the road through tearing eyes. I looked sideways at him and giggled. We roared. I laughed until I couldn't breathe, the skin on top of my head tightened until it tingled, and tears blinded my eyes. Each of us would try to stop, sucking our lips closed, and then explode again, setting off the other one. M gasped out, "Imagine explaining geese guts all over the front of this thing," and we convulsed again. Half an hour later we regained our control, our bodies weak from the spasms.

Our hysteria had shattered the stiff politeness between us. The next day, I struggled to direct M to the gas pumps, while he intermittently snarled out the driver's side window at me. No apologies came forth from either side during the quarter of an hour that it took him to pump an ocean of gas into the RV. We climbed back inside the camper and began to fight without reserve.

"How can I help you if you won't listen to my directions?"

"You have no concept of what I'm trying to accomplish. Why don't you drive this thing?"

"You know I said I'd learn."

"Right. When hell freezes over."

"What do you mean by that? How can you say that?"

"What do you think I mean? You seem to know everything. Why don't you guess?"

"You're impossible. Impossible. I can't believe I've agreed to do this. I'm not gonna live through it."

"Well, I'll just try to improve myself, to live up to your standard of perfection."

My control dissolved. He roared, I screamed. I teetered on a precipice, losing my balance and mentally flailing my arms. He accused me of condescension, of speaking to him like a child, of telling him what to do. I accused him of a complete lack of appreciation for my efforts, of treating me like an incompetent. We struck at each other with the special fury that boils up between treasonous partners. Finally fatigue and breathlessness lowered and slowed our voices. My throat felt scratchy. M said in a flat tone, "I'm so angry I've got butterflies in my stomach."

"Then you have to calm down before you drive." My rage slipped into terror at the thought of riding next to a maddened driver. We began to let each other complete our sentences. Battle fatigue brought on almost conversational tones as we spoke of our mutual resentments of the other's nagging, condescension, and criticism. We asked each other for some acknowledgement of our small gains in competence. By the time we swung back out onto the road, exhaustion and perhaps some small sense of restored understanding had calmed my insides. We left our tipsy dance of accommodation in tatters on the tarmac of that rest stop. Hopefully we were headed out onto firmer ground with each other. We'd find out.

M at the Mystery Spot

3

Adrift

Sodus Point, New York, needles eastward out along Lake Ontario's southern shore for a mile or so, to form the northern boundary of the state and the country with its left side and enclose Sodus Bay to its right. We were camped at the edge of a dairy farm in Junius Pond, twenty miles south of the lake. Suffocating July humidity blanketed the rolling hills, and the sun glared determinedly in the sky every night until after eight o'clock. Picnic tables at each campsite stayed empty all day, as everyone retreated to whatever air-conditioning their rig offered. Mild claustrophobia threatened. One evening M suggested a drive, and we headed north up Route 14. Ahead of us, black clouds began to roil the heavy blueness at the horizon.

Farm country drifted past our windows. I had spent the first decade of my adult life in Brooklyn, where I quickly learned to dismiss upstate New York as irrelevant. Now its unimagined prettiness softly stunned me. A small brown and white sign read "Welcome to Lyons." Languid figures stood about the soft ice cream stand. Youngsters darted between parked cars, couples flirted at the curb, and older figures sat on front steps fanning themselves. They were all African-American and all strangers in a place that I'd never heard of before. The small surprise of this unimagined place sharpened my sensation of being suddenly very far from home. We continued north, our car windows sealed against the heat.

The road dipped and twisted through the hills, then swung around a long curve to reveal churning gray water just beyond the houses of Sodus Point. The figures outside our car were a mix of skin colors now, wearing bathing suits and waist-wrapped towels as they meandered through streets empty of cars. Two blocks into town our windows rattled, and straw hats went tumbling down the street. Light flashed from an unseen source, and one or two people began to hurry. We nudged along a beachfront block and turned into a neighborhood of large white houses set on spacious lawns. The clapboard siding echoed New England seashore architecture, but something in the details, a different turn of railing, a strange roof line, reminded me that I was not at home. These affluent houses gave way to smaller summer cottages crowded around the perimeter of another beach. A spiky line of lightning cut the sky in front of us, and thunder boomed simultaneously. People began to run, mothers calling to barefoot children, teenage girls shrieking into the wind. I watched from inside my vehicular cocoon, safe and dry, an aging mother put out to pasture by her own grown children.

Rain slashed sideways against the car, obliterating our windshield view. The road dips filled with water as we crept out of town through deserted streets. South of the lake the downpour straightened to a vertical curtain that overwhelmed our windshield wipers. Then without fanfare the natural drama abated, and M began to drive a little faster. We laughed over the sudden attack and retreat of the storm. Ahead of us ragged clouds drifted apart, revealing behind them a sky washed to pale blue.

The storm echoed my emotional life. One moment grief would overwhelm me as I contemplated the paucity of life, the next moment giddiness over the beauty of the world would blow through me. A sensuous day could pass, from a thigh warming bike ride in dawn's pale chill, morning hours lost in an Edith Wharton plot, lobster for lunch and slow afternoon sex. Twilight would fall and bam! Depression would grip my throat and hollow out my chest, leaving behind the conviction that my remaining life promised only a succession of hours of longing and days of grief. My moods swung inexplicably, eroding any sense that I might control my own emotional life.

I developed techniques for soothing myself. Pretty magazines were my drug of choice, the glitziest home decorating ones that I could find. I fell into trances over photographs of living rooms filled with pale upholstery and darkly curving mahogany furniture, diaphanous curtains billowing out over open windows that guided sunlight onto crystal vases loaded with roses in luscious hues. I studied articles on decorative painting and daydreamed about the walls of our condo done up in stucco or faux marble. Mentally, I chose two tables at home to paint black and gild at the edges.

And there was food to comfort myself with: breakfasts of eggs and sausages, or bagels and smoked fish, lunches of lobster or shrimp or clams, pastas with home made fresh herb sauces. There were afternoon ice cream cones, dipped in sprinkles, or served in a cup with hot fudge sauce. Five o'clock cocktails came with specialty cheeses like a blue veined Gorgonzola or a squishy Brie, pepperoni sliced thin, marinated vegetables, three kinds of crackers, and a medley of olives. We dined on grilled steaks or fresh fish, bread from local bakeries, a vegetable mélange, and homemade pie or pastry shop cake. Fantastically, my weight stayed steady. Perhaps the laws of caloric intake had been revoked, along with so much else that had previously constricted me.

If a few days had passed since we shopped, leaving the refrigerator partially empty, and I'd read my last magazine, late afternoon would bring a slight lump into my throat. I would think, I am not myself. Sure, I could read a novel and make a big pot of pasta with jarred sauce and lots of cheese on top. But neediness would squeeze my chest, reminding me of my homesickness at boarding school decades ago, or my worst days of premenstrual agony in the years since then.

My fertility was officially behind me. My periods had sputtered out over a few years. I hardly remembered the era of heavy menstruations, the weeks of cramps and bloating, the hot flashes, mood swings, irritability, and periodically a strange out-of-body sensation. For the last couple of years I had gloated some over my ability to pass through this transition without the ubiquitous hormone replacement therapy. I loved the freedom of even keel months, unmarked by cycling dates. When a woman gives up measuring out her months by week count, she regains a control of time lost decades before in pubescence.

The first time on the road that I felt the achy twinge of cramps in my lower belly, I thought, indigestion. Then the exhaustion, the headaches, and the bloat set in. Could this be? A friend of mine had menstruated once every two years all the way through her fifties. I rushed out and bought the necessary protection at the closest drugstore. Nothing happened, and in a couple of days the feelings passed.

Three weeks later, the same screws tightened in my abdomen, except now I also got weepy. From his years of observation, M suggested that I might be cycling without actually menstruating. Hormones were bouncing around, doing their stuff inside. Perhaps they were regressing in the face of the strain of the road. Or perhaps these symptoms of renewed fertility had something to do with my determination to change my life. But these observations come in hindsight. At the time, no such analogy formed in my addled brain. I felt knocked off balance, not myself in yet another way.

We puttered along from campground to campground, all of them filled with vacationing families. Late in the afternoon, parents and children meandered by our rig, returning to their campsites from swimming and ball games. Memories of our own young sons, and the irrevocable loss of that time, threatened to shut down my breathing. Empty nesting, you might say. But my two boys, son and stepson, were over thirty by now. The bittersweet loss of their constant presence had been immediate more than a decade ago. The winter that my son first left home I had spent days in half-crazed bargaining with an imagined deity, offering to trade five years of my life for one week to share with his eight-year-old self. I had confessed these desperate internal negotiations to a friend, herself a mother. Her eyes widened and she touched my arm with the grounding pressure of one who fears for another's sanity. "You need to stop this thinking," she urged.

The same deranged sense of loss that now returned wasn't the first sign that some demented process had seized hold of my brain. My obsession with creativity had been growing ever since I stopped working a salaried job. All through the late winter and spring of that year intermittent nocturnal panics struck me, centering on the fear that I would NEVER ACCOMPLISH ANYTHING. I would awake full of the terror of death and lie staring at the ceiling, my heart fluttering in my throat. Mark would be gently snoring beside me, oblivious to my discovery that my life was effectively finished, and that my last years were to be given over to meaningless trivia. In the dark I'd contemplate my coming loneliness and gasp at my casual severance of all work and social connections.

The last six weeks at home these frights had disappeared, absorbed into the flurry of planning and packing. But once on the road, the aching loss of my sons and the terrors about my future threatened to destroy all hope for the future, or even any rude proficiency in coping with daily life. I sat in my camper and brooded over the view of families sashaying by. Little children dragged beach towels in the dirt as they tottered after their parents. Young mothers and fathers in a languor of fatigue encouraged their offsprings' progress down the road. I wanted to shout at them: Savor this! Treasure it! Now you move in packs, never alone. You may imagine the luxury of solitude, time to think of only yourself and not the children. But sooner than you expect, all this will evaporate, and you'll be like me, sealed on the other side of the glass, eaten with envy. At the age of fifty-seven I had reduced myself to an old crone at her windowsill, no longer a part of the world outside.

So here I was, obsessed with the loss of my children, experiencing some sort of phantom biological fertility, fearful that my ability to create anything was gone for good. Maybe it was the road, or perhaps my fairly total inexperience in fashioning a life that was not ordered by the daily demands of job and family. It would certainly be inconvenient to go mad, out here on the highway. Yet all those zipping swings from a sense of crushing loss to breath-catching euphoria and back again unhinged me from any sense of sanity. Marooned on the surface of North America with just one steady companion and only the most nebulous of itineraries, what did I expect? I had cut so many ties. I could only blame myself for my loss of mental stability.

M hadn't known what to expect either, but he was often strangely elated. He seemed hardly able to believe that he had talked me into this wild scheme. He developed a prodigious appetite for sightseeing. In Rome, New York, we wandered about Fort Stanwix, listening to guides discuss the French and Indian War and watching families romp and droop in the heat. Near Niagara Falls we took in the American Falls, the Great Lakes Garden, the Maid of the Mist boat ride, the Aquarium, Terrapin Point, the butterfly museum, the flower clock, the theatre at Niagara on the Lake, the Horseshoe Falls, the Cave of the Winds Tour, the…oh, you get the point. Finally I wrestled him away from the area, and we headed into Michigan, tottering up I-75 through the grueling heat, aiming for the Upper Peninsula. The whole state was drying out into long rolling hills of dun colored grass, punctuated by stands of dark evergreens rusting to brown at their edges.

In spite of the sweltering weather, M pressed forward in his attempt to visit every site that published a tourist flier or posted a road sign. Before this trip, I was the entertainment director of our relationship. During our working years, what drove M out of the house on weekends was plain restlessness, more than a desire to do any particular thing. He loved recorded history books, TV, the Rolling Stones and any Italian singing he could find on Napster. He'd grown up more athletic than academic and spent some years wandering and pursuing different careers before earning his BS degree at age forty, transforming himself into a muscular computer geek. The Internet offered endless amusement to the political junkie in him. He started his days at home at the computer and ended at the TV, surfing back and forth through history and science programs.

Many nights on the road we had little TV. The only program we pulled in with any regularity was Fear Factor, and watching bug-eating marathons quickly pales as a way to relax after hours of driving. As for the Internet, most campgrounds would let us plug into their phone line to pick up our email, but that was it. The man who used to react to my entertainment suggestions with indifference suddenly became fascinated by any possible location marketed to tourists. We visited every waterfall on the map in upper Michigan, and there are lots of them. In St Ignace, Michigan, we spent forty-five minutes at The Mystery Spot, a series of rooms built on a slant in order to convince you that the laws of gravity had been suspended at that spot. Eight dollars apiece, please. Tourist trap it may have been, but the suggestion that gravity is not necessarily an element to count on mirrored my own state of mind at that moment. A family of four boys, aged eighteen to three, and their attractive, friendly parents shared the tour with us. The mother had that cheerful competence that can surround a lucky woman in such a situation. The three-year-old danced along the beams set askew and staggered into his father's arms, tossing us all into laughter. For half an hour M and I were part of a family again. But it was only illusion, along with the site's deliberate distortion of physical perceptions.

During another day of driving about, we stumbled on the Civilian Conservation Corps Museum in Grayling. The buildings still stand where the young recruits lived, left much as they were when those inner city toughs inhabited them in the 1930s. As we browsed through the old newspaper clippings and handwritten letters, a man arrived and began to tell the park ranger that his father had been the first to propose the idea of the CCC, in a letter to his senator. He offered copies of the responding letter by Senator Driver, which thanked the citizen for his idea and promised to bring it to the attention of the Committee on Military Affairs. Pride in the documentation of his family's recorded role in American history swelled in this visitor's voice. M and I hovered nearby, enjoying this glimpse of archival expansion.

So M went on finding places to explore, and I went on following. How had it come about that now I was the one who looked for chances to stay sedentary in the camper, when he was so eager to go, to get out, to bike, to sightsee? It was discomfiting. Long ago I'd decided that my husband has a somewhat depressive character. He leavens it with humor and anger, but up until this year we both knew that I was the resident optimist, while he was the pessimist. In brighter moments we appreciated the strength of such a union; in darker moments we each lamented the burden of enduring the other's distorted attitudes. But now the familiar equation had turned topsy-turvy. I was irritated at his cheerfulness and confused by my own irritation. After all, for years I had wished him to be more enthusiastic for life. Now he countered by worrying out loud that he had somehow forced me into this trip. No, no, I told him. But couldn't we just be still for a while?

The symptoms of menstrual cycling and the other ailments that I managed to develop, of colds and headaches and stomach upsets, sometimes kept me in the camper with a book, while M shot off on a bike ride. He might be gone an hour, leaving me in lovely solitude. On such an afternoon, slightly cooler for a change, the air-conditioning turned off and a breeze coming through the window, the cell phone rang, and an unfamiliar feminine voice asked for me, using my childhood nickname.

"Trixie? This is Suzanne. Suzanne, your cousin."

"Hi, Suzanne!" Surprised at her voice, I started rattling on to my cousin in San Diego about our travel plans and the possibility of our making it to southern California. She cut me off in mid-sentence.

"Trixie, my father died. We found him in his garden this morning. Do you think you could call your mother? My daughter is in labor, and I, I…"

"Oh, of course." What a bumbling idiot I was. The next thing this experienced social worker said was worse. "I guess you just don't know what to feel right now." Suzanne had the grace and good sense to end the conversation, leaving me to call my mother and tell her that her younger brother had died. At least she was not alone in her house in northern Vermont, but spending the week with my own younger brother and his family on Martha's Vineyard. In the last few years so many of her contemporaries in the family had died that a certain routine had been established. Because my parents were originally from California, most of the funerals took place there. Mom bought a plane ticket for one or two of her children to represent herself at these funerals. In the beginning, I would return and offer Mom a description of the rituals, a kind of attendance by proxy. She wasn't interested; she didn't want to listen; she changed the subject. She was life oriented and rarely expressed much grief as the deaths picked up speed. I used to think this somewhat cold, but it was her survival technique in the lonely universe of aging, a necessary toughness if one is to keep going. So I expected some similar reaction from her in this case.

My uncle had been an affable and distant figure in my life since my childhood. The continental separation between his family and ours limited intimacy between my cousins and me. I knew that he and my mother spoke regularly by phone. Their visits had stopped half a dozen years ago, when both lost the strength for the thirty-five hundred mile trip necessary to see the other's face. Two years previously, my brother and I had attended my aunt's funeral. Once again, my mother had been matter of fact in the face of this event. Tough old broad.

I dialed my brother's phone number. He informed me that his wife had taken Mom out to lunch, and we agreed that he would give her the news when they returned. Later that evening I called again, just to check in. He told me, "She's taken it kind of hard." My nephew ran to take the phone to her.

She was sobbing. My mother, the stiff upper lip, self-made Yankee, choked on her words. For the second time that day I found myself on the phone with no idea what to say. "I'm the last one left now," she quavered. "My whole generation is gone. It's lonely, you know."

And all I could think to say was, "I know. I know, Mom." I promised to call again the next day, offered to do whatever she wanted about the funeral. Her response was incoherent. Her brother had taken with him all the parallel memories that no one else could share. Her loneliness shamed my own sadness.

My children were still here, available by phone, living their lives, in place when it was time for a visit. Their daily presence might have passed from my life, but they were still part of the same world. Our shared experiences, even with all our contradictory understandings, still connected us indivisibly. My own brothers lived on, native speakers of the code talk that evoked the prismatic memories of our childhoods.

My uncle's death sent me into a contemplative mood that mitigated the depressions and wild mood swings of the preceding weeks. By the time we left Michigan and descended into northern Wisconsin, my emotional feet had found firmer ground. The challenges and pleasures of each day came at me with less desperation and disorientation. Please let there be some confidence coming back to me, I'd think. M's newfound joyful attitude didn't irritate me so much now. Maybe I could do this traveling year after all.

Re-enactors at Fort Stanwix

Dudley-do-right and Me, Niagara Falls

4

Finding the Current

Two people had set off on this trip. There was me and there was M, my quotidian intimate of twenty-seven years. To some extent I had survived that closeness by erecting psychic privacy corners during our decades together, and he must have also. I accepted his perceived transparency as a daily necessity, only rarely glimpsing the shadow of a stranger living in my space. By the time of the trip, our boundaries for trust and privacy had been hammered into flexible but resilient parameters. All that carefully constructed wedded certainty was about to go up in smoke.

We headed down the road, hours and miles moving by outside the fiberglass walls and inside our brains. We rode mostly without talking, listening to wind and motor noise in between the strains of Andrea Boccelli, Janis Joplin, Crosby/ Stills/Nash/Young, the three tenors, Sinead O'Connor, Brahms, Eros Ramazatti, Paolo Conti, and the bagpipes of Scotland. In the weeks before departing M had plumbed Napster for a music store's worth of CDs.

M drove. I knit. I kept my fingers going and my gaze out the side window at passing fields, forests, billboards and buildings. Mostly I ignored that white line running past our right side wheels. From time to time I would glance leftwards at M's profile, baseball hat pulled low on his forehead, mouth set, gaze shifting between side mirrors and the road. He had difficulty sleeping the nights before we made long drives. I'm a great sleeper, but early in our relationship I had been introduced to M's insomnia when it came accompanied by nighttime cluster headaches. His groans would rouse me from somnolence to an attempt to comfort him. The headache might subside almost as fast as I could come to consciousness, and we would sleep until the next one came. At least, I slept.

Cluster headaches don't have the same name recognition that migraines do. "My migraines" is the way Mark referred to them when we first met, or just, "the headaches." He'd been having them since early adolescence. I was introduced to them on our second date, when he came to pick me up at my apartment in

Brooklyn. We sat in the basement kitchen chatting with my roommate, until he suddenly excused himself and disappeared out onto the sidewalk. The roommate and I watched his legs pacing back and forth in front of the stoop and shrugged at each other. New men were always a puzzle. In fifteen minutes this new man returned, apologetic, explaining he'd had a headache, but it was gone now. The puzzling moment passed, forgotten in the scintillation of a new relationship.

I would discover that many of his headaches lasted longer, up to forty-five minutes sometimes. During their turbulent confusion he would abruptly stalk out of the room. As we got to know each other better, he began to stay with me and seek comfort. My soothing techniques didn't really work. I'd try holding, stroking, speaking softly. He would leap up and start an agitated pacing, groaning and swearing. Sometimes he pounded his forehead with his fist, and I would jump to his side and try to distract him. This didn't work, and he would writhe away from my touch, challenging my whole sense of being both a new girl friend and a social worker. As quickly as the headache came, it would subside. We would touch again, and I'd feel reassured. Once a day occurrences of this sequence were manageable. Nocturnal episodes, breaking sleep sometimes two or three times in one night, were worse. And then there were the times when the headaches came like rolling thunder, four or five a day, more at night, for weeks at a time.

I had believed since childhood that with enough information, I can solve any problem. I read everything I found on migraines. M's headaches seemed different from the descriptions I was reading. They were shorter, for one thing. He didn't want to lie down; in the throes of one he didn't want to stop moving. He refused to see a doctor. He said he'd seen doctors in his youth, and they never helped. Once or twice I did browbeat him into seeing an MD, but the physician seemed more concerned about the dangers of pain medication than the reality of M's pain. M left these appointments convinced that his only course was to tough it out. We'd puzzle together, trying to identify pain triggers. Perhaps it was stress, anxiety, anger, or ambivalence. None of our theories ever bore out consistently, and the headaches continued their capricious entrances and exits. His father had suffered similar cycles for many years, to watch them mysteriously disappear in middle age. He had also toughed it out.

One icy winter we were living in Berkshire County in Massachusetts, and the headaches became unrelenting. Weeks of pain and constant exhaustion began adding up to months. Unremitting nights of broken sleep weakened me, moving me past sympathy to desperation. I asked the psychiatrist at the mental health clinic where I worked about new migraine medications. He suggested a neurologist in Pittsfield. Unable to muster the energy to resist, M agreed to an appointment.

Dr. S. walked into the examining room wearing an open lab coat over the nineteen-eighties Berkshire County professional uniform of wide cords and flowered tie. He glanced at Mark where he slumped on the examining table, heard two descriptive sentences of his complaint, and nodded. "Yes, that's classic cluster headaches you're having." He showed no sign that he suspected M was seeking narcotics, and he never asked a question about M's mental status beyond the headaches. The agony was as real to him as to us. Gratitude weakened my knees. The medication that he prescribed brought relief to M for many months. We had found a hero.

Eventually the power of his pills waned, and M went back to cycles of pain and periods of relief. We moved to Boston, where we made the rounds of doctors who regarded my husband with suspicion and suggested a lot of testing but no treatment. Finally another doctor believed in his pain, a woman in the neighborhood hospital, and moved quickly, as Dr. S. had. For several years she treated M with a series of medications, each successful for a while until it slowly lost its power. We went on living around the ebb and flow of his pain. Then, in his early fifties, the headaches echoed his father's pattern. They became scarcer and faded away.

Cluster headaches shaped M's life for forty years. Their malevolent presence intermittently ruled our lives for the first two decades that we were together. They must be counted as contributors to my husband's wildly gyrating ambitions and consequent unstable financial status throughout his early adulthood. They undoubtedly amplified the development of his pessimistic temperament. They surely honed his quick, wanton wit, his ability to make almost anyone laugh. Through humor we survive what we must, coming sideways at the oppressor, distracting, mocking and belittling its power.

Why we choose whom we marry is one of the greatest questions. "Who am I?" "What am I doing here?" These questions pale beside the one we fairly regularly link to our spouses: "What was I thinking?" M's headaches hooked my nurturing side, but his humor drove me crazy in the beginning, bouncing me between hilarity and indignation. He made light of everything, including how seriously I sometimes took myself. He mocked himself until my sides ached. My own skin slowly thickened, and I learned to tease back, in defense and because it was fun. More fun than I'd had in a long time.

When M hazards an answer to the question concerning his selection process, he mentions my steadiness, my determination, and that constant effort to comfort. For the first years of our life together, he would have mentioned them only silently to himself, while we battled outwardly for ascendancy with our differing approaches to adversity. The most important challenge we shared was the fact that we each had a son, in a time when few people were having babies. The terror and joy of being parents to these four-year-olds drew us together, at a time when most of our contemporaries were childless. There was so much less explaining to do in the beginning of our relationship, about the commitment that a child brings. Most of our first dates involved attendance at a Saturday afternoon puppet show, or a museum art group equipped with crayons and paste, or the biggest playground we could find. After a series of boy friends who'd had no idea what to make of my son, sharing a G rated matinee and tubs of popcorn as a foursome was more fun than the trendiest restaurant visit.

We progressed from instant parents to major struggles about what that meant in terms of commitment. We married, moved around, and slowly built increasing stability, trust and understanding. The little boys grew up and left us. No more family camping trips: we two were on our own. When we had announced our intentions for this trip to friends and colleagues, their reactions ranged from disbelief to enthusiasm. After M described our plans to a woman coworker, she fixed him with a look of baffled concern and asked, "Does your wife know about all this?" I think it probable that some of our married friends developed a small betting pool on whether our union would survive the year.

M did think that he had persuaded me into the plan, somewhat against my inclination, and he worried that it might backfire on him. I saw the whole decision and process as mutual. But he was the force behind it. Just as I had been the force behind buying our first house and deciding to start investing for our retirement, this whole journey wouldn't have happened if he hadn't been dead set on doing it.

So here we go, he in low slung baseball cap, me with clicking knitting needles, moving out along the waters that border the northern edge of our country: Lake Oneida, Lake Ontario, Lake Erie, the gorgeous convergence of Lake Michigan and Lake Huron, and finally, Lake Superior. The thick birch forests crowding the shore at Paradise enchanted me, and Pictured Rocks National Lakeshore provided challenging hikes to view the cliffs that overhang Superior's choppy freshwater ocean. Even in the heat, the air blowing off the water smelled of northern tundra. Grand Sable Dunes sit at the eastern end of the National Lakeshore. Signs along the hikes here describe the role that grasses play in the gradual reclamation by plant life of sandy areas. I read every sign and examined the topography, fascinated by grass, that toughest of plants. Something surely was happening to my mind, if I could watch grass growing with such pleasure and patience.

Fayette State Historic Park, Michigan

M on stage at the Opera House

We began to slant westward along the northern edge of Lake Michigan. The chatty campground owner in Rapid River, Michigan, told us about nearby Fayette Historic State Park. The heart of this park is a cluster of empty buildings scoured clean by light and air. They comprise a Jackson Iron Company town that flourished for a quarter century before dying in 1891. During those twenty-five years, according to its brochure, "the blast furnaces produced a total of 229,288 tons of iron, using local hardwood forests for fuel and quarrying limestone from the bluffs to purify the iron ore." Five hundred people at a time lived there, immigrants from Canada, Europe and England, speaking several different languages as they labored at the pig iron furnaces, kept house, raised their children, organized socials, attended worship services, and mounted productions in their modest theatre. Parts of the furnaces and the docks, rows of workers' houses, the Opera House and the school still stand. The graciously proportioned supervisor's house, wrapped with a porch, sits apart on a hillside. The stage in the Opera House supports a carefully rendered backdrop of a sylvan scene portraying a river strewn with dead tree trunks. Down the path from the Opera House lie the collapsed ruins of the church. Exhibits in the cavernous Visitors' Center present census lists from the eighteen-seventies and eighteen-eighties, filled with German, Polish, Italian and English names, indicating married couples, their children, and single men who boarded with the families. Everyone in the town appears to have been in their twenties or thirties. When the company lost the profit generated by the confluence of water, iron, wood and limestone here, the plant closed, and these people moved on. Over a hundred years later, Mark and I wandered nearby in our RV and visited the remnants of their world. I wondered if they were sad to go when they left here. How many scattered out across North American and how many returned to Europe? Some probably feared for the future, and some looked forward to greater riches. One imagines the women packing the families' modest belongings, then groups of adults and children boarding the trains, the boxy wooden buildings left behind to stand silently curing in the northern light.

We headed down the western shore of Lake Michigan towards Two Rivers, Wisconsin, planning to visit my cousin in Manitowac. Dropping south on Route 41, M pulled our rig into a dusty turn off for a brief rest stop, next to Spies Athletic Field. We were in the town of Ocunto, or maybe it was Pennsaukee, or perhaps Brookside. A thick cement gateway, embossed at the top with 1937, opened onto a field of long grass. A radio played over a distant loud speaker. Was this field still alive, like Lyons and Sodus Point? Or was it slipping backwards into history, like the CCC camp and Fayette? No matter, we drove on.

A week later, still exploring the unimagined Midwest, we walked the Mississippi Mile in Minneapolis, crossing the Stone Arch Bridge where Mary Tyler Moore had flung her wool beret into the air of her new life every Saturday night on early seventies TV. The Sunday we were there the heat was deep and still, and we had the place to ourselves, with the exception of an occasional spandex clad jogger. Below us, a huge, narrow lock, miniaturized by distance, slowly filled with water while a sight seeing boat waited at its far gate. Cascades cut the river, reminders of the wild power that remained in spite of the muscular industrial buildings and the well-groomed greenswards on its banks. On the far side of the river, tucked up near the lock and dam, the exposed interior walls of a half dozen broken buildings crowded silently against the vertical bank. Like evidence of earlier success at taming the river, now overbuilt by the modernization of those efforts, this site seemed to be settling under our gaze into the realm of archeology, disappearing from view to molder below the living level. At some unspecific time in the future, experts may seek to reconstruct our present day reality from its fragments, by then well pulverized by the weight of earth. Or so I imagined.

Imagination. Always there, called into service over and over here in the Middle West, where I had spent so little time before. Until this year, I had hardly differentiated between Ohio and Minnesota. Now the solid reality of the heart of the country, with all the spaces and details between cities, challenged our previous habit of categorizing our nation by east coast and west coast. We kept stumbling on places that had never entered my conception, places that proceeded to establish themselves in my memory and tease my thoughts. One such place was Roscommon, Michigan.

On Michigan's Upper Penninsula

We had been on our way to the Upper Peninsula, worn out with driving. Woodalls Campground Directory listed some places near a river with canoeing available. The chance of a day's break from driving enticed us. I called the larger of the campgrounds listed to check availability. Yes, they had a site. Name, address and credit card number, please. On hearing the Massachusetts address, the pleasant feminine voice said, "Oh, my husband grew up there, a place called Northfield." I shivered in surprise. I had spent four years of high school at Northfield School for Girls, something I rarely mention to anyone. Telling people that my formative adolescent years were spent at an austerely religious and proudly intellectual institution that restricted its enrollment to girls and sought to identify itself as the educator of preachers' kids and teachers' kids, while also instructing its share of the elite's offspring that attend New England boarding schools, well, it took just too much explaining. But a thousand miles away, startled at a stranger's mention, I instantly identified myself as an alumna. "I don't know exactly when he was there, but he sure talks about it a lot," his wife remarked. For the rest of that afternoon's drive the man who remembered Northfield occupied my thoughts. He was probably much younger, since he was male, and the school had only gone co-ed a couple of decades ago. I felt oddly nervous.

After supper that night we headed for the campground office, M with laptop computer and plans to retrieve our email, me with trepidation and curiosity. A tall, slim man, grey haired in a premature manner, sprang out of the door as we arrived and greeted us. "You the person from Northfield?" Indeed. "Then you knew my father." I squinted at him, no idea what he was talking about. "My father was the chaplain." The school had provided an intense religious education, moralistic, intellectual, and non-denominationally Protestant. Every week we attended bible study twice and chapel six times. I had done this for four years. At that moment, in dusty north Michigan pinewoods, I had absolutely no memory of the chaplain. Blank slate. This man and I had indeed overlapped in time at the school, but he was the young son of the forgotten chaplain, still clearly proud of his father. He stood there rattling off the names of different buildings and personnel at the school. Nothing he remembered overlapped with any of my recollections, which centered on the insides of the dormitories, the girls who formed my social clique, the strict schedule of bells that marked forty-five minute periods from awakening until lights out, favorite and feared teachers, the homesickness of my first two years there and the excitement as vacations approached. Within five minutes, this man and I had sorely disappointed each other. He turned away to go and eat his supper, and I hung around M at the phone line, where he was downloading our email. I felt a fool in not being able to match this man's memories at all. Only days later did I realize my own disappointment at his inability to match mine. We shared this bit of esoteric history, but we shared nothing, not even the same mental map of the place. The places that the man had mentioned evaded my own recalled topography, but memories of high school continued to wash through me for days. I wrote to my senior year roommate, whom I hadn't been in contact with for a few years. She was the only person who might appreciate this encounter in the hot mid-western dust, and her memory map would closely overlap mine. If my letter reached her, she would have no way to contact me, but I could picture her laughter and surprise. For a few days we held imaginary conversations in my head.

The breadth of the continent, experienced mile by mile with wheels on the ground, provides a lot of time to daydream. Wool gathering, my mother called it. I reminisced at leisure about my adolescent anticipation of life, and about how far I had diverged from those expectations. Middle-aged musings, strung out over the luxury of long hours in the passenger seat. In a recurring dream that has visited me since my twenties I am living in an apartment at the top of a high building, a place filled with light and wrapped with terraces, the only view the blue and white of sky. This dream always suffuses the next day with optimism and peace. One night in Wisconsin it came, dropping off its message of freedom and pleasure, lifting my mood towards the future. Yes, I was pleased with present circumstances.

Certainly my husband was happy. We were moving every day, and his morning started with detaching and storing all our lines, wrestling the tow bar into place, hooking up the car, then checking the tires all around. Every day he completed all this with cheerful determination. He's a good guy, but chores around the house, wherever we had lived, had invariably brought forth some complaining. Deep in early morning dew, hosing out the sewer line, he never even muttered. He really wants to be here, I thought. Well, so do I.

Mike, our long distance service manager, had scheduled an appointment for us in Minneapolis, to replace a rear panel on the RV that was torn off in an encounter with a large water pipe during the course of an overly confident exit from a New York campsite. When we got to the repair shop we discovered that the manufacturer in Alabama had shipped the wrong part. No matter, we were glad to have come this way anyway. M wanted to visit the Mall of America. He had some of the corniest places on his year's list of things to do. Thing was, his kid-like pleasure in them gave zest to sites it hadn't occurred to me to wonder about. When we were done with the Mall and Mississippi Mile, we rolled south on Interstate 35 and then west on I90 towards Mitchell, South Dakota and another of M's sites.

Mitchell held the Corn Palace. We planned to park the RV as soon as possible once we left the Interstate and negotiate the town by car. We were unhitching the car in the parking lot of a supermarket just off the exit when a half grown boy in tee shirt and shorts shot across the pitted pavement directly at us on his razor scooter.

"Where you headed?" He inquired.

"The Corn Palace." I smiled. He squinted at me.

"Oh."

"What's that DakotaFest over on the other side of the highway, anyway?" I was curious about the fields full of tents and trucks we'd spotted nearby. Here was someone who could tell me about it.

"It's for farmers. We're not farmers." He shrugged. Eagerness flattened to caution in his eyes. He dangled his scooter, shifting his feet irresolutely while we secured the RV. I tried to keep the conversation going by asking him about the upcoming opening of school. He muttered noncommittally and pushed himself on his scooter slowly out across the empty parking lot. He had sought from me a detailing of distant destinations. California, at least, or maybe even Alaska or Brazil. Our land yacht had loomed up next to his prosaic food market, offering the chance to converse with explorers. And what were they interested in? The Corn Palace! That stupid farmers' fair. This boy itched to follow his dreams out of this prairie town.

My own curiosity was closer to the ground under my feet. Something was settling down inside of me, steadying my gait. I felt easier with my husband, with his startling enthusiasm for sightseeing, his roaring libido, his perpetual good cheer. On we went, poking through the middle of the continent, encountering places and people that we'd never considered the existence of before, looking for advertised and un-advertised sights, months to spare stretching before us. The pleasures of freedom, time and relationship were slowly taking hold of me.

The Corn Palace in Mitchell, South Dakota,

5

Horse Country

A battered 24-seat school bus clattered into the dirt yard and jerked to a halt, throwing a choking cloud of dust over M, me and a dozen other tourists. We climbed aboard. Two Indian men mounted the steps last, the only riders without cameras or binoculars slung from their necks. The driver twisted his bulk away from the steering wheel to greet us. "Hi, folks, I'm Norman. I'll be your guide for the next three hours. You got questions, fire away. I'll see if I have the answers. Here we go."

He headed the bus at a good clip back down the long rutted driveway, away from the Visitors' Center of the Wild Horse Sanctuary, south of Hot Springs, South Dakota. Bodies slammed up and down in the worn out seats. Norman suddenly jerked the steering wheel right, sending the bus straight up a prairie incline. We would not see a road again for almost two hours.

The bus swayed back and forth, threatening to tip over, its windshield pointing straight up at the blue sky. Then Norman tramped on the brake, and we jerked to a slanting standstill. He killed the engine and stepped outside to gather a fistful of dry plant material. Or rather, he dragged his twisted bulk down the bus steps and back up them. With swollen, arthritic hands he gently split the plants into two bunches to pass amongst us. It was sage, one of three distinct kinds that he would show us during the afternoon, each with a slightly different, sharply sweet smell. I was dying to see the horses, but Norman was fascinated with every detail of life here on this high prairie at the edge of the Buffalo Gap National Grassland, right down to the plants under our tires.

He wanted to show us not only the life now present in this rugged land, but evidence of the life that had previously passed by. His body's mobility might be severely handicapped by arthritis, but he handled the bus with swift aplomb as we headed for a distant cliff. While our vehicle jounced across the prairie, he regaled us with his doctor's recommendations. "Stay in bed, he says, you need to take care of that back. But hell, what am I going to do in bed, at my age? I'd rather be out here. So what the doctor don't know won't hurt him." He delivered this speech in a tobacco-roughened voice and then roared in laughter, so pleased to have bested his doctor.

By now, we could see numerous irregular cave openings in the approaching cliff. Up to about the height of six feet the outcropping was scratched with designs: stick figured humans and animals, abstract arrangements of triangles and star bursts, initials, whole names, numbers and dates, and a few cryptic messages: Don here 4/14. Six horse. Norman claimed that some of the petroglyphs were ten to twelve thousand years old, while other chiselings had been carved in the twentieth century. The cliff's protective caves thrusting above the unforgiving prairie had attracted humans for thousands of years, and the evidence of this lay before us. Since the site was not preserved in the chain of national and state parks, successive visitors freely piled their decorations on top of the messages of previous passers-by. Until the land was bought by the Institute of Range and the American Mustang and incorporated into the Wild Horse Sanctuary, the rocks collected the carvings of whoever happened along with a sharp instrument. Later in the summer I would compare this carefree process with the carefully guarded ancient messages at El Moro National Monument.

Back into the bus we climbed for another joint bruising ride to a high, flat area, the crown of a series of cliffs that dropped away to a sere valley. Centered in this area stood a tall tree, towering over the low vegetable life that clung to the prairie floor. Long cloth streamers tied to its polished branches were slowly shredding in the wind. More multi-colored cloth, gathered into lumpy balls, encircled the trunk. Igloo shaped structures fashioned from pine branches clustered nearby. Norman twisted around in his seat and addressed the two silent Indians at the back of the bus. "Would you like to talk about this place?"

They peered uneasily out the window. "No." We were gazing at the site of the annual Sun Dance of the local Sioux. According to Norman, for a long time the white government outlawed the yearly gathering, so the Indians practiced it clandestinely. When the Institute bought the land, it invited the tribes back to dance openly, for as long as they wanted. At this point in Norman's speech one Indian suddenly warned, "I wouldn't take any photographs," and then sank back into morose silence. Norman told of being invited to watch the beginning of the ceremony the previous year. "I tell you, the flames, the dancing and singing, it was something. Before the piercing started, we were asked to leave. They are dead serious about all of this." Piercing? Weeks later we would see painted depictions of this in the Charles Russell Museum at Great Falls, Montana. Indian males stabbed daggers through their chest skin and attached these weapons to the central pole tree, to dance around it in blood and pain.

The man in the back seat of the bus who had warned us about using our cameras stirred again, apparently compelled by the guide's remarks to accept his obligation to impart the accurate truth to a group of innocents. Without directly answering Norman's questions, he offered his own commentary. Yes, he attended the Sun Dance, but not every year. He had never participated in piercing. A man pierced himself after the completion of a year lived under a vow. Every year the Indians talked about not having the ceremony the next year. "Then someone submits a vow and it's held again the next year, has to be." His tone conveyed respect, irony, and resignation in equal measure. I turned away from gazing at his profile, fearful that my horror might show in my eyes. M had been snapping photos out the window while the Indian spoke.

We left the Sun Dance site and ricocheted away across the prairie's irregular hillocks and fissures. In the middle distance stood a group of horses, noses pushed down into the spiky grass. The bus slammed along directly toward them. A few horses calmly raised their heads to watch our approach. Three reclined indolently on the hard ground. Shouldn't they run, frightened off by this rattling yellow bus hurtling straight at them? Norman halted about fifty feet away. The horses held their ground. Only two things scare these horses off, he explained: helicopters and ridden horses. Men used these devices to chase and trap them in the wild. The horses know that yellow buses just carry figures without ropes, figures that stand nearby and gaze at them. Similar jalopies bring humans who drop off hay or other treats. It was okay with them if I wanted to stand twenty-five feet from the herd and watch this equine mix of brown, roan, black, and gray. They moved in leisurely grace, grazing, watching us, grazing again. Round of body and short of leg, they wore their health in their contentment. A pretty paint foal, vividly splashed in brown and white, stalked among her elders, peeking at us over bent backs and under concave stomachs. Norman told us how a rich man from Los Angeles had recently purchased this beautiful youngster. Soon she would leave the prairie and ride off in a trailer to a life in a paddock, becoming the pampered pet of a young girl or a rising star of the racing circuit. But most of the herd would live out their unbridled lives on this prairie and die a natural death here, protected and provided for through the benevolence of the Institute.

Several years of a serious drought had the Sanctuary struggling to balance their philosophy of natural freedom for the horses with some measured help to enable them to survive. Even in this desolate area, land developers had moved in, buying up tracts and eliminating grazing rights on their holdings. The resulting lusher grass, unchecked by animal teeth, provides easy fodder for lightning strike fires that don't respect legal property boundaries. To offset the results of these fires and the drought, the staff supplied the horses with molasses tubs and extra hay. So the herd had probably hoped that our approaching bus brought these provisions. When we turned out to be only a group of camera-wielding tourists, they went back to their full time job of grazing. Only the beautiful foal, destined for tinsel town, evidenced any lingering curiosity about us.

Time to go. I would have stayed much longer, standing in the dust, watching these creatures, imagining their rough coats under my palms. But Norman had a schedule to keep. The horses raised their heads to watch the bus leave, and then one of them wheeled and slowly trotted away. He must have been the leader. The rest of the herd left off their grazing and followed his slow lope, their manes and tails flowing out over rippling backs, hooves thudding across their prairie sanctuary.

Horses endear themselves to humans on a regular basis. I have loved them from a distance ever since I can remember. They played a vital part in the mystery of my parents' past, that time so compelling and so unbelievable to offspring. My mother told the story of her first glimpse of my father many times to my brothers and me, but its coincidental magic never dimmed. "I went riding once a week. It was the one luxury that I allowed myself. One day, at the stable, the owner said to me, 'Let me introduce you to someone.' Your Dad stuck his head around the corner and said hi. The next week he called me up and asked me to go to the circus with him. Six months later we got married. Imagine if I hadn't been taking those riding lessons!"

My parents were Californians, rooted in the west and all its enchantments, including horses. My father came from inherited money, but my mother's parents were of modest means. Before they spent their honeymoon at the Grand Canyon, she had never been past the state's eastern border. When my father brought her to see his family's summer home on the New York side of Lake Champlain, she fell in love with neighboring New England, and they spent most of their married life in Maine and Vermont. Here they spoke fondly and frequently of their western roots throughout my childhood, creating a mental landscape of rugged mountains, deserts, and horses.

Of course, horses live in eastern stables also. There was a riding academy of sorts a few miles north of our home in Vermont, and when I was twelve my dad took me and two of my brothers there on Sundays for a while. My brothers were given ponies and sent out to circle the paddock on their own, but Dad put some effort into teaching me proper riding skills. Sit up straight, he'd tell me, hold the reins in both hands, down low. Now give your horse a little kick, to get him going. That's right. Lean forward, not backward. Keep your knees tight to his sides, keep your heels down. That's right. I teetered along in pride and fear on that enormous beast, while my father hovered gracefully on his own mount.

The lessons stopped when I went away to boarding school. Among the items I packed was a carved wooden statue of a roan colt, neck arched, feet planted in a broad stance, that my father had bought for me at Marshall Field's in Chicago. Forty-five years on, I still have that horse. His tail and two legs have broken off repeatedly and been glued back, each time the wood growing more powdery with age. He's still beautiful in spite of his glue-encrusted fissure, a constant reminder of my father's love and my childish imaginings of his west.

Wild Horse Sanctuary, South Dakota

When M and I got to South Dakota in our RV, we entered that west of my imagination. The vast territory between California's eastern border and the farm-land of the Middle West evoked my childish dreams. These visions featured snow capped mountains, deep rocky canyons and rolling prairies sparsely peopled by horseback riders, all generously influenced by the western movies of the nineteen-fifties. Badlands National Park looked something like all this. So did the Black

Hills, with their sharp mountains crowned with rocky promontories and flanked with dense evergreen forests. The smell of the tinder air, the fierce heat of sun on head and shoulders, and the hundreds of brown bison sharing the fields with pronghorns, deer, eagles, and prairie dogs, matched my childish ideas. This place still suggested the Wild West, somewhat tamed by man's presence but harboring a remote heart inaccessible to the age of the Interstate.

One place in the Black Hills that humans have, of course, rather spectacularly reached and shaped is Mt Rushmore. Our evening visit evoked powerful musings of centuries hence, when the monument will lie in ruins, the reason for its existence lost to human memory. What will sentient beings then make of it, as they examine its humanoid faces and imagine the effort required to create them? Walking up the broad, dark slope towards the evening light show, surrounded by a flickering crowd more felt than seen as they shuffled past the curb lights, the crisp outlines of the Visitors' Center and the rows of amphitheater seats crumbled away out of my reverie. Time slid by, like those skyscapes in movies that depict the passage of days with racing clouds, stars, sun and moon. While we waited for the evening's presentation to begin, eons proceeded through my mind, the solid sidewalk dissolved under my feet, and new beings in a fantastic future climbed towards this strange monument, murmuring to themselves about why a civilization would bother to build such a thing. My fantasies distracted me from any interest in the presentation about the four stony presidents above the heads of the darkened crowd. While spotlights moved in shadowed drama over the sleek facial planes, and the guide spoke of the enormous feat of engineering that created this panorama, I lost myself in my own daydream of Rushmore as a future Stonehenge, cloaked in mystery about its purpose and design. When its clear intention was lost to history, would it become a protected site for the reverent regard of future tourists, or would it molder alone, but for the occasional passerby's personal graffiti?

Introspection was becoming one of the chief delights of the trip. Long hours on the road lent time for daydreaming back and forth in time. The blue-gray wool of my knitting crept through my fingers and wound into cables and ribbing that lengthened out into my lap, while the Interstates' yellow lane lines flowed by outside our windows. The choppy emotional seas of the first weeks had smoothed out into calmer depths where I could snorkel for hours contemplating the submerged past. Still, an occasional storm of frenzied thoughts about the future roiled through. My journal pages during these weeks record random affirmations of a continuing attempt to set the shape of my future. "I feel determined to do what I want to, no matter what." "My creativity is in privacy." "I am in control of my own life."

Riding with my father, about 1960

So I kept declaring this determination on the page to be active, not passive, to achieve not just to receive. But I hadn't much of a clear idea what I intended to do next. M and I had gotten used to constant physical and mental elbow bumping, and we'd developed techniques for keeping corners of psychic privacy. M could watch TV in the front of the camper, while I closed the folding bedroom door, plugged earphones into the CD player, and floated away on Schubert, or let Mozart spin patterns in the background while I lost myself in a Dorothy Dunnett novel. My original reading plans for this year had included a list of serious books about the history and cultural development of the English-speaking world. Those books remained unopened while I sank into the self-indulgent sort of reading that had comforted and contained me since I was eight years old and huddled under the blankets with a flashlight and <u>The Little Colonel</u>. Ms. Dunnett's thick layers of allusion and her swashbuckling action transported me to medieval Europe from our foam core bed, thirty feet from the fiberglass wall of the next camper.

As we sank deeper into the west, I continued my indulgences in escapist reading, familiar music, and wandering daydreams about both the past and future. The affirmations in my journal evidenced a continuing drumbeat of desire to live differently when we got home. All those panics in the black spring nights had meant something beyond just nervousness about breaking patterns and getting ready to leave. Or so I hoped.

Most of the accomplishments of my first fifty-seven years had been driven by necessities created out of the actions of others. Starting at age thirteen I'd spent two years overcoming my wrenching homesickness at boarding school. By sending me there, my parents launched me on course to leave behind the secluded world of their Vermont town. Over a decade later, when my first husband walked out and left me with a four-month-old baby, I provided for the infant and myself by returning with serious intent to my nascent career in social work. The four years alone with my son created a dogged vigilance in me over his and my financial safety. Married again, I continued to work, finding job after job as we moved about the country. No one else's paycheck could be trusted. My career moved forward, more as a function of my overdeveloped conscientiousness than as a result of conscious ambition. M has frequently accused me of workaholism. Maybe. I was never very good at blowing off a boss's directives, perceived or explicit. My mother once said to nine-year-old me, her eyes full of love, "I never have to worry about you. You always do your homework." She delivered this commandment as she turned away from exhorting one of my brothers, none of whom ever seemed to have any difficulty in putting something, anything, before school. Her eyes shone down on me in brief gratitude, as she created the mantra that thrummed from then on into my adult life: always do your best when others expect things of you. I am what some have called a good employee

I take a somewhat perverse pride in that characteristic. I never surrendered it throughout the 'do your own thing' days of the sixties and the 'be here now' times of the seventies. Before I met Mark, I played at irresponsibility in group therapy discussions and weekend parties, when my son was visiting his father. But Sunday nights I was always there, back on duty. So M's siren song of irresponsibility when we first met hooked me. He was a thirty-one year old drop out from the business world, driving a taxi at night and radiating an egocentric freedom. Of course, it was a big fake, contradicted by his commitment to his son. In an unguarded moment during our first months together, he announced to me that guilt is a very good reason for doing something. Guilt! It was 1974. Our generation was supposed to have expunged ourselves of such an inconvenient feeling. And if we needed help to do this, we had psychotherapy and street drugs.

So there we were, meeting each other's friends, establishing ourselves as a couple and a study in contrast: working, single mother and hippie, carefree, divorced father. "Mother" and "father." Therein lay the real dynamic of our beginnings, beneath the superficial differences. We battled over issues of career versus work, loving your child versus disciplining your child, believing in the future versus living in the present. The harder we grappled with each other, the closer we grew. I struggled with M to get him to strive more in the present for a benefit in the future. Yet the catnip of his resolute irresponsibility effervesced our daily lives.

He didn't acknowledge it, but he was not so sure that his devil may care, chuck it all attitude was just the right one to guide the rest of his life. He stuck around with conscientious me, got a real job, met my mother and threw himself into raising our boys, all the time obstinately calling himself a hippie. We continued spending a lot of energy on a mutual refusal to accept the other's weightings of responsibility, future, and security. While we struggled time passed, both boys reached first grade, M and I married, and we all moved across the country. Now officially step-parents, M and I kept up our emotional wrestling over ideas of living, at the same time we paid bills and went to school conferences and took our kids to Disneyland on weekends. Somewhere during the first decade our voices just died down, leaving behind only an occasional flare-up. The battle had sunk into irrelevancy.

But I'm rambling, like my thoughts out on those highways. The daily tasks of camp set-up and break-down, small repairs to the vehicles, and sightseeing choices were puny intellectual challenges compared to the mental demands of child rearing during mornings and evenings sandwiched around a work day spent in relentless problem solving amid endless office politics. For years I slogged through exhausting weeks of such days, barely making it to the inadequate relief of the weekend, very occasionally trying to raise mental eyes to some conscious diversion before returning to the fray. Fatigue circumscribed any attempt at activity not dictated by my responsibilities to a host of intimate others. After our sons left home, the habit of hard work only redoubled my efforts at the job.

When we hit the road all those encumbrances faded away as quickly as the circular scene cut in an old movie, leaving behind a staggering disorientation in the first weeks. By the time we reached South Dakota we had found an easy rhythm for establishing and striking camp, negotiating necessary chores like grocery shopping in unfamiliar towns, and organizing local sightseeing missions. Beyond these simple duties stretched the mental freedom that I had dreamed about way back when M and I had first met.

Temperament and habit prevented me from focusing just on the present. The shape of tomorrows and the possibility of any achievement in them haunted my musings as we wandered west. What was left of my own future lay before me, beguiling, demanding, thrilling, and frightening. From my springtime midnight panics, I had progressed to some nascent determination that an additional series of meaningful chapters laid ahead of me. I clung to the tremulous resolution that my achieving life was not over. I didn't want to settle into being just a consumer; finished with contributing. I was struggling with relevance, or meaning, or maybe just anxiety. So what came next? I didn't have a clue.

We all cart around constructs that we've distilled from observing our parents' attempts to create order in their own lives. We tuck away in our mental attics myriad observations of Mom and Dad. Our direct surveillance commences sometime in their middle age, as we reach the age of consciousness. We add to this all the stories of their youth they either tell us directly or leave for us to discover. Around the time our own age starts to parallel the phase of their lives when first we noticed them as individuals, they begin to grapple with old age. My own mother, after raising four children and burying her husband, studied history and developed advanced skills in a changing array of handicrafts. She also oversaw the building of three new residences for herself within the span of fifteen years, each one further north in Vermont than the last one. My father-in-law, after a long and distinguished career in the New York City public school system, retired to Florida with his wife to enjoy a life of leisurely pursuits and detailed reading of the daily New York Times. I had more of my mother in my ideas about our future. M had more of his parents in his ideas. We fought some about these differing expectations during the trip. After all, this year was a test drive of our lives together without salaried work. He would speak happily of a future in Florida, or I would speak happily of a future of achievement, and off we'd go on a jerky, irritable conversation about our coming years. It was as if the struggles over hippie and conventional life styles had been resurrected in some sort of incipient geriatric version.

We headed north, into Wyoming and on towards Montana, settling into a driving rhythm that chewed away at the miles. We were bound for Canada, traveling up across the eastern plains of these two states that are better known for the mountainous regions in their western halves. Hours rolled by over the pavement, punctuated by stops at highway rest areas. In the afternoon, while M took a break from driving and napped on the bed, I'd explore the anonymous rest stop, watching other travelers come and go. I could milk a thirty-minute walk from the equivalent of two city blocks of sidewalks. If the state had thrown up an historical marker, it was significant entertainment. Then we'd be off again for another couple of hours of driving before pulling into an overnight camp spot. So we progressed northwest through Rapid City, South Dakota; Cheyenne, Wyoming; Casper, WY; Sheridan, WY; Billings, Montana; finally turning off the Interstate system to strike due north on US 89. M's birthday passed, marked only by a supermarket cake that I managed to find in Sheridan and present with a weak flourish after hamburgers and salad. I thought he might mind the lack of celebration. I thought I might mind. He didn't, and I didn't. The trip was upending previous priorities.

Dun colored prairies rolled away all about us, fading into the atmosphere to suggest an ephemeral horizon line against a distant sky. The daily repetition of measureless space floated me into a vaguely narcotic euphoria. Near Springdale, Montana, where we turned north on US 89, the prairie had started rising up into foothills on our western side. Route 89 carried us to US 12, which guided us to Helena, where we picked up I15. We were crossing back and forth over the Continental Divide, tracking the Missouri River's blue-black waters bordered by tender green shoots that sprouted like miracles in the surrounding brown. Passing the Continental Divide signs in the clear air, the land rolling deeply into the distance ahead but buttressed on our left by sharp, mountainous profiles, I seemed to float just above the earth, gliding through the atmosphere untouched by the RV's vibrating ride. Thus one afternoon I was knitting and dreamily watching the river twist past us, when a gust of wind caught the rig and knocked it sideways, banging me back down to earth. I glanced at M. He yawned a couple of times and shook his head, as if to reawaken himself. Maybe we needed a break.

6

The Function of Wounds

We had traveled steadily for three days since leaving the Black Hills, trundling along at sixty miles an hour. Woodall's listed a KOA in Great Falls, Montana, where we could stop for thirty-nine dollars a night. We were in the habit of paying twenty-five dollars. "That's steep," I said to M.

"I need a break," he replied. We headed east off the Interstate onto a road lined with strip malls and tire dealers, an unlikely neighborhood for an overpriced campground. When we turned at their sign we discovered that the dreary commercialism was only one building deep. The access road to the KOA struck south into open prairie for half a mile before reaching the main gate. In the office a homesick young military wife from Pennsylvania checked us in, explained that the high fee gave us free admission to the attached water park, and talked longingly of green eastern fields. We followed her directions into a grove of trees clustered on a rising swell, surely an unusual sight on this sere grassland. The fluttering foliage of the deciduous trees created a porous screen, through whose flickerings one peeked out at the hypnotic distances of the prairie. At dawn and twilight, the trees provided a magnet for hordes of birds, who descended to socialize and eat, ignoring the proximate humans. Gray and white woodpeckers with black markings around their eyes, dusky birds shaped like robins except for their squared off and yellow banded tails, red cardinals, small brown sparrows and larger blue-black birds inhabited the tree branches, trilling and uttering sharp commands, hopping between branch levels and performing curving flights at the trees' perimeters, oblivious to our delighted presence. By the time morning sunshine stood hot and steady over the plain, forecasting the day's true heat, the birds had disappeared to some mysterious resting place to await fading twilight, when they would return and repeat their show for us. Their cycling arrivals and departures punctuated the enveloping beauty of this place. M got out his bike and took solitary rides around the campground and down the dirt paths that wandered off into the prairie dust. I arose before dawn to walk those paths and watch the red sun break over the horizon. Evenings we sat side by side in canvas chairs and allowed ourselves to be hypnotized by the dance of our fire against the tree trunks. Happiness poured down my insides like warm water.

The third afternoon there, the cell phone chimed as I lay reading and awaiting the evening arrival of the birds. It was my son. We'd been on the road for about six weeks, and the horrid longing for my children that had tortured me had abated somewhat. During long Interstate days I still devoted some time to musing about my failures as a mother, or to mournful contemplation of the inevitable but devastating separation from adult children. The voice of my son, Chris, on the phone always brought a bolt of joy. But this time the joy fizzled fast.

"Ma, how would you feel if we went to my in-laws for Thanksgiving instead, this year? They are planning a special celebration for Uncle Patrick." Let me explain that as far as I was concerned Thanksgiving belonged to my corner of the messy network of divorced and in-law family structures that surrounded my son and myself. We all traditionally descended on my mother's house in a four-generation gathering around a meal that my brothers and I prepared with haphazard glee. Every other holiday throughout the year was up for grabs, but not Thanksgiving. I already had plane tickets to return east in November. I choked into the phone.

My disciplined practice pursued over the years, of cultivating an acceptance of my son's independence and of conscientiously recognizing how his married life had increased his constellations of relationships and obligations, fractured in an instant. Since he reached his manhood I had resolved to avoid the struggle for control that had dominated my relationship with my own mother throughout my twenties. That resolve now took flight in the clatter of a racing heart. "No, no, that's not right." My voice trembled; if I stopped now I wouldn't dare to go on. A young child may fear a parent's desertion, but by his maturity the tables turn, and the parent inherits that yawning vulnerability. I shook with the fear of it, but I sputtered on.

He reneged. Quickly. The conversation found its way to safer ground: his job, his children. We reaffirmed the Thanksgiving plans and hung up. I should have felt relieved. But anger had gotten hold of me and kept rising up through my chest in overlapping tides. The dams carefully built over the years, meant to confine my love for my son to manageable dimensions, had been shattered by his one tentative withdrawal for the holiday. From our canvas chairs, M and I watched the light go to gold, fade to blue, and then deepen through purple to black, while I ranted on. M listened. Most times my husband is a man of action, a take control guy, impatient with any lengthy analysis of a situation and with no small ability to quick anger himself, whether in his own defense or of those he loves. He doesn't like to discuss emotional matters; he wants them solved and done with. But that evening he just listened. Perhaps I was paying my dues for so many years of disciplining the expression of my emotions, for what my mother used to call a lack of passion in me, for what M has described sometimes as a difficulty in reading me. It seemed that being on the road had thinned my protective shell and left it easy to crack. The pain only got worse as darkness thickened around us.

Bedtime came. I couldn't sleep. I dozed and thrashed, then awoke completely around two AM and lay brooding for hours. I wanted to get the lump out of my throat, I wanted to either cry or lose the need to, to just stop thinking. After all, I'd won the day, and we'd all be together for Thanksgiving. So what was my problem? When the window shades softened to gray I finally slept, awakening exhausted three hours later.

Anger flooded back in with the taste of coffee. Chris would be at work by now. I dialed the phone before I could compose my first sentence. For so many years I had prided myself on being a mother who accepted her son as an adult. Now this mother was calling him at his office to complain and demand. Friends used to tell me stories of nagging their children, and mentally I'd raise a contemptuous eyebrow. Get a life, I'd think to myself. Don't be so silly, so weak. But on this morning, I had gone over to the other side. "What have I got to lose?" I said to M.

Truth is, I thought I had a lot to lose. If I didn't, I wouldn't have spent all those years in carefully controlling my expectations, in measuring expressions of my needs in our relationship. That morning, if I'd stopped myself to think, I would have known that I believed that the sum total of my son's love for me was probably on the line. After all, he was the one who was young and vital, starting a career, a family, and a record of achievement. I was the one who was graying, moving away from achievement to leisure, from relevancy to extraneousness, from being needed to needing, growing faintly ridiculous.

It's axiomatic that parents love their offspring with a pure passion that the child can only return tinged with ambivalence. The child's slow struggle for independence requires along the way a snarling of the ties of affection to the parent. What we hope is that our children pass our fierce love down to their own children. As the next generation of tiny dependents comes onto the stage, our own position in life's ebb and flow shifts also, foreshadowing a returning dependence. God, I hated that. My refusal to accept this fueled my anger at my son that day. I could let him achieve independence, but I despised being put in the position of needful supplicant. This is not where we had started out, after all.

Like all first time parents, most of my personal freedom evaporated abruptly at his birth. While sleep loss and roiling hormones still had me reeling, my first husband walked out, and in a blink I was alone with this baby. Many nights we were two lost pilgrims, except that I was the one who could walk and talk and had the responsibility for his survival as well as my own. Within that lonely wilderness we formed a society of two in love and commitment. He knew nothing else, and I permitted nothing else. Nobody dented that company for four years, until M and his small son came along.

Offspring reach adolescence just as it's dawning on the parent that the status of their own youth is in serious question. The celebrated milestone of forty is followed by the less heralded ones of forty-one, then forty-two, then etc. Your child's body is stretching up, getting angular, growing hair. He's keeping more secrets and turning away when he used to turn towards you. All this is good: the goal, after all, is his competent independence in the world. But what parent doesn't feel some anger, remembering the sweetness of the preceding love and the familiar habits of sacrifice? Forget those bromides about unconditional parental love. They are insufficient for calming the frustration and anger of the honest parent of a teenager.

Every parent finds a way to weather this transition. Myself, I dealt with it by welcoming back my own freedom, trumpeting to my friends the delights of a household of just two, and the relief of not having to await the return of errant sons at night. Lord, how a person can lie to herself. If I had let myself feel more loss when my children left, maybe I could have avoided all this pain, the gloomy contemplation of young families in campgrounds across the country, the plunges into depression during our first weeks on the road, and now my disorienting rage at my son's contemplated desertion at Thanksgiving. Maybe.

Chris answered on the second ring, business-like tone. When he heard his mother his voice turned welcoming, not defensive. I pushed forward anyway, saying all my nocturnal imaginings about being slighted, disrespected, deserted, forgotten. His own voice cracked upwards. "After all, you're the one's that's traveling." But I kept going, like a caricature of a demanding mother dredging up the past, recalling the times other plans had been cancelled, his absence at events on my side of the family. And then he said, "It won't happen again, Mom. I didn't mean to hurt you." The phone slipped around in my damp hand, and my knees wobbled where I stood. The lump came back into my throat and then slid away on a swallow. I had made myself vulnerable to him as never before, and he had arisen to the challenge. We had climbed over a wall together and started down another path. In the end all that was left to say was, "I love you," and "I love you too."

I hung up. It was ten in the morning. I had no sense of time, or of what to do next. Thank God for Mark's sightseeing instincts. We drove out to Ulm Piskkin, an ancient buffalo drop that now anchors a Montana State Park. A dusty half-mile trail leads out to models of Indian huts close by the cliffs where an Indian brave dressed in a buffalo hide blanket would lead the herd to its death over the edge. From there we went to view the paintings of Indian piercings at the Charles Russell Museum. Our last visit of the day was to the beautiful bubbly spring that Lewis and Clark discovered for white men here. We wandered through the day, taking in the sights, and I kept talking in fits and starts, and M kept listening.

Highland Games, Canmore, Alberta

7

Prelude

The undulating plains along the Montana/Canada border shape the fierce winds that pour off the mountains to the west. Distances that appear modest on the map turn into marathons that suck up hours. The giant air currents toyed with our rig, lifting it from the pavement, shaking its sides, and banging it back down. We made three hundred horrid miles the first day out of Great Falls, Mark gripping the wheel while I clutched knitting needles and tried not to shriek. At twilight the wind dropped as we approached Okotoks, Alberta. Here we spent the night among vaguely unfriendly Canadians.

In the morning I misread our atlas and guided us straight into downtown Calgary, which resembled the financial district of Boston, only worse. Building walls drew closer and closer to us while pedestrian overpasses crisscrossed our windshield, within inches of our height limit of eleven and a half feet. After an eternity in this morass, M swearing and me squinting desperately at the traitorous map, we struggled free without sustaining any physical damage and made our way westward to the town of Canmore, exhausted from tension. It was Sunday. I called my mother, who exclaimed, "You're right where I want you!" This was a disconcerting greeting for a progeny who had struggled for so long not to do what her parents expected of her. It seemed Mom had some friends in Canmore, a British couple who had lived for a time near her in Vermont.

"I'm going to give you their number, you must call them." It's the kind of maternal instruction I had avoided following since adolescence, but in the spirit of doing things differently this year, I rang them up. They were small and round, spoke with crisp British accents, and lived in a modern house on a street cut into one side of a sharp cliff. After a tour of the town and its former Olympic facilities, they took us home for tea and hot biscuits. The developer who'd built their home had lined up a dozen houses on this incline, where they could catch the sunlight and view the town's night-lights. My mother's friends had established an English garden of delphiniums, roses and daisies in their small yard. This cozy couple in their late seventies seemed more like natives of Kent, England than New England transplants in Alberta, Canada. The son they'd come to live near in Canmore had just moved away in search of better job markets. No direct sign of sadness about this broke through their cheerful hospitality, but once the mother peered out her car window and remarked, "The mountains aren't friendly. I argue with my son about that. They are not entirely beautiful. They block the sun. I liked the mountains back east better."

I agreed with her. These hard grey beasts with their threatening edges exhilarated Mark, while I scrunched into the car's passenger seat, peering morosely out at their aggressive beauty. Cold settled down into the corners of the camper and the soles of my shoes. One day we paid forty dollars apiece to perch in a Snocoach as it crunched over the Columbia Icefields. The enormous beast of a vehicle crept up the glazed incline on treads, while the guide/driver talked about moraines, crevasses, hundred-and-fifty-year-old water, and the toe of the glacier. The characteristics of this landscape that fascinated my fellow bus passengers were differentiated only by their degree of gelidity. I regretted not bringing mittens. During the twenty-minute stop at the glacial toe, M wandered happily about the icy surface with the other tourists, while I huddled in the coach and sat on my hands.

Twenty-seven years ago, the two of us had camped through this area during the first summer of our relationship. We were traveling on a tight budget in a faded blue Gremlin, its hatch back packed to the gills with tent, sleeping bags, cooler, propane stove and lantern, pots, and clothing. It was July when we reached the Rockies, and I don't remember minding the cold. I was falling in love, and our air mattresses and double sleeping bag served us fine. We ate canned soup poured over sliced bread for lunch and hamburgers for dinner. Back then, Banf was a tiny mountain town with shops offering trail maps of the mountains and serious outdoor gear that we couldn't afford. Jasper, further north, was even more romantically remote, with its central train station and alpine architecture. Hippie travelers in bell-bottoms and tie-dyed shirts lounged on the grass outside the Visitors' Center. Patchouli incense perfumed the air. The long whistles and trailing smoke clouds of the black trains that pulled through the central station evoked a distant, western yearning. We hit town thinned and hardened from our cross continent tent travel and sought out the free activities. The only entertainment we paid for was a visit to Miete Hot Springs, where we brought our own towels and lounged in the sulphurous waters along side Midwesterners.

That was 1974. This was 2001. That was a time when I only intermittently phoned my mother and would have recoiled from a request to visit an old friend of hers. This was a time when I called her every Sunday and tried long distance to include her in our travel. Our conversation often dipped into reminiscing. "Oh, Jasper!" she cried. "Your father wouldn't get off the train. He was afraid of how the altitude would affect him." My parents had been aboard one of those dark trains in 1944 with my two older brothers and the infant me, moving west from New England months after my father had experienced his first heart attack. "I got out and stood on the platform," she told me. "The train, the mountains, it was so romantic." A young mother in wartime, anticipating widowhood, stands alone in a strange train station and thrills to the setting. She had this perverse optimism, or maybe it was a useful difficulty in accurately grasping one's circumstances.

A recurring dream visited me, in which I was driving on the Icefields Parkway, holding a book on the steering wheel and reading at the same time. An exit appeared and I took it, descending the ramp before I looked up, suddenly scared of what I'd been doing, driving so fast and not looking at the road. What did I think I was doing; where did I think I was going?

We had arrived at Canmore in the midst of the annual Highland Games. Men competed with bagpipes and in games of hurling massive tree trunks. At night everyone gathered in an open tent to dance, sing and drink whiskey. We sat at the crowd's edge, enjoying the party. Then we moved northward, to Banf, Lake Louise, and on to Jasper. He loved it. The nightly cold made me stiff and edgy. The government campgrounds were full, in spite of the weather. Near Jasper we had to spend our first couple of nights in a parking lot that served as an overflow to Whistlers' Campground. In the morning the frost stiffened the scrubby grass at the edge of the pavement. I shivered at the dinette table and crouched over my first coffee, staring at the side of the camper next to us and wishing we could leave, while M rhapsodized about the smell of the air.

The mid-morning alpine sunshine vanquished the frost and softened my disfavor for the area. The rivers of this country were gorgeous bands of thick turquoise water, concealing their depths beneath gleaming opacity and breaking into storms of glittering sparkles at their rapids. Local minerals, rather than a reflection of the atmosphere above, create the water's coloration. The blue-green torrents cut through a landscape of yellowy grasses and mountains shading from navy to plum against a cerulean sky. Sometimes the night cold brought snow dustings on the higher peaks, blunting their ferocious edges with flashing whiteness. I liked them better then.

One day we repeated our jaunt to Miete Hot Springs, to sit in the reeking pool listening to conversations in German and Japanese. We rented extra towels and luxuriated in the abundant heat. In the parking lot herds of small mountain goats wandered about cleaning up the pickings. The deciduous woods shimmered in shades of gray-green and gold. We lunched on fresh mozzarella, smoked fish, roasted veggie salad and peach tarts from a deli in Jaspar.

Mark's mood skidded from exhilaration to giddiness and back in the course of each day. After a couple of nights in the parking lot, we had gotten into the regular Whistlers' Campground. Here we kept our curtains open to admire the elk herds wandering amongst the campers and tall pines. Signs posted about the place warned of bears and suggested that it was wise to make noise while out and about, as the bears really didn't want to come upon a human, any more than the humans wanted to meet a foraging bear. The chance of an ursine encounter gave my daily walks an edge. Red berries stained the fresh bear scat on one of the river trails. I sang to myself while I walked this trail, old songs remembered from childhood. Camptown Ladies. Red River. When Johnny Comes Marching Home. Tunes that my mother had taught us from a battered songbook illustrated with faded line drawings of people cavorting in pre-World War One costumes. Other families were turning to television in the early nineteen-fifties, but not ours. Instead, my mother spent hours every day entertaining us with songs, board games, croquet, badminton, and more. Almost fifty years on, those tunes popped into my head, and I tramped through the lodge pole pines and croaked them out in a loud stutter, letting the bears know that there was a dangerously off key human being to avoid.

As for the elk, they were in rutting season and couldn't have cared less about our presence, as long as we didn't get between a male and his herd of female intended. If we did, (and of course Mark did, with camera in hand,) the male lowered his enormous candelabra of weighty antlers and stalked forward, starting with a whistling sound that moved rapidly on to a threatening chortle, a cacophony produced with trembling flaps of neck tissue. His females continued grazing, unconcerned about the show of male dominance, but we retreated to the inside of our camper. Almost every campsite here had a rig parked on it, but the campground resembled a ghost town left behind by a previous civilization of RVers. No one wanted to take on those triple chinned male elks. Once or twice a day the staff would sally forth waving ten-foot poles decorated with bright streamers and empty soda cans. They'd advance three abreast on the elk colonies, shaking their poles, reclaiming for mankind this small piece of real estate. In a gratifyingly ridiculous retreat the male leader of the herd would tuck his tail down against his rump and crash away through the woods. Eventually his females would pull their heads up out of the grass and follow him in desultory resignation. Every display of this collapse of testosterone-driven bravado in the face of some used aluminum and torn paper reduced me to giggles. Mark was amused, also, but he didn't convulse as I did, each time our brave staff defenders, armed to the teeth, came into view. I guess it wasn't a guy thing.

Whistlers' Campground, Jasper, Alberta

We had decided to stay here longer. Rather, M had been lobbying to stay longer in the mountains. After we got to Whistlers, I agreed. Partly it was the wild animals and pine-scented air of our campground. Partly it was our proximity to Jasper with its trains and decent restaurants. Partly it was the complete absence of TV reception, lending a deep quiet to the evenings while I immersed myself in Vanity Fair, Martha Stewart and Brahms' Violin Concerto. I was feeling agreeably happier and gladly consented to stay an extra week.

In spite of the explosion of gift shops and art galleries since 1974, Jasper retained a distinct emphasis on outdoor sports activities. From the array of choices, we picked out a day of fly-fishing instruction and practice. Our instructor/guide, Danny, picked us up at 7:30 at the gate to Whistlers, provided us with hot coffee and thick ham sandwiches, and drove us in his bouncing jeep out past Jasper to a broad valley bisected by one of those dazzling turquoise rivers. We were going to try our luck here. But first we had to practice. We spaced ourselves out in a field and began to rehearse flinging the tiny weight on the end of our line into long, reaching arcs, trying to match Danny for aim, length and grace. It was the sort of activity that a year earlier would have bored me with its repetitive, deceptive difficulty. This day, as my shoulder gradually stretched into the task, as the advancement of the sun prompted me to shed my heavy jacket, as Danny introduced exercises designed to increase our accuracy, a beneficence settled on me. Time passed slowly, and I inhabited every gentle minute.

After a couple of hours we climbed back into the jeep and headed for the river. Our reward for our morning of training was to play along the edge of that jeweled water, balancing on the rocks that tumbled along the riverbank and pretending to see what Danny saw out among the sparkles. There was more wind here, and the water's dancing lights blinded me. I wiped away tears and struggled with knots in my line. Danny talked about seeing a fish dart by and about the possibilities of the quieter pool of deeper water fifty feet away, while I crouched over my knotted line and hoped that on my next cast I could at least see my hook sink into the water. Danny caught a small fish. Mark fluttered his lure out over the deep pool, testing the possibilities. Sunlight moved over the jade water, sharpening the shadows of the rocks. My tears abated, and I watched my lure flicker through the current. When Danny said it was time to go, I wanted to stay on in the polished air and wait for sunset.

On the way home I sat in the jeep's back seat and watched the fields of golden grass bounce by, rolling away toward the mountains' evergreen clad feet. Back at the camper M and I spoke happily of the day and decided to sign up for one of this outfitter's two-day jaunts. We'd learn to fly-fish, gain a hobby we could share. Pleasant fatigue overcame our elation, and I cooked a steak and salad supper. The elk had gone elsewhere this evening, and the campground was still, as darkness gathered on the ground and moved up the mountainsides toward the luminous sky. It was Monday, September 10, 2001.

Snow Coaches on the glacier

8

Out of Our Control

I floated up through the last veil of dreams to an awareness of the warm weight of the quilt and the sounds of Mark rustling around at the other end of the camper. His movements must have roused me. My mind thick with sleep, I stretched out my arms and legs in the snug spaciousness of the bed and sniffed at the scent of coffee. On the radio a man spoke in a slight Canadian lilt, just loud enough to hear.

"We have a report that a plane has struck the World Trade Center in New York City."

"What? What did he say?" I sat up and reached for jeans. "Did he say a plane?"

"That's what he said."

"Oh, it must have been a private plane, some small plane. Remember the time a man scaled the side of the Trade Center?"

"It wasn't that. He put a tightrope between the two buildings and walked it."

"Yeah, right. Crazy."

"French."

"Must have been a cone head." We chuckled over the old Saturday Night Live reference, and M turned up the volume. CHED out of Edmonton continued with news, weather and traffic reports. A warm and sunny day was predicted, Celsius 24 would be reached. Traffic on Route 16 coming into the city was becoming heavy near the St. Albert Trail intersection. Provincial officials had announced an inquiry into safety concerns on the Trans-Canada Pipeline, and pipeline officials were stating that safety was their highest concern. An arrest had been made in the beating death of a local prostitute. Alberta Government Services was investigating improper practices by funeral homes, as a result of numerous reports filed with the Calgary Police Service. Police were currently engaged in a standoff with a man in the city's north end, who was reportedly holding a woman and child hostage. Shots had been fired, but there were no reports of injuries yet. The owner of the sawmill in Grande Cache confirmed that the company planned to close the sawmill, which, it said, had been losing money for years. Town officials had expressed concerns that such a sale would destroy the Grand Cache economy, and they requested assistance from Provincial authorities in negotiating with the sawmill's owners. The local reporting continued for forty-five minutes, frustrating but reassuring. I drank coffee and ate a cup of blueberry yoghurt. Once we heard the follow-up on the New York report, we could proceed with our day.

At eight o'clock, the newscaster returned to the story. The second plane had already hit. The Edmonton announcer's measured monotone continued piling up reports in his northern inflections: collapse of the first building; other planes reported down; the US Capital had been hit; unconfirmed report of bombing at the Pentagon; the second Trade Center building collapsed; another explosion had rocked New York; whereabouts of the US President unknown.

Our son lived on East Ninety-sixth Street and worked in midtown Manhattan. I dialed his cell number, "just to check in," I told M. An angry buzzing answered from the satellite. I waited a few minutes, tried again. Same buzzing. I pushed the redial button again and then again, faster and faster. Panic began squeezing my breath. I went out to the pay phones in the campground, holding feet that wanted to gallop to a stumbling walk over the rutted dirt. Stay calm, stay calm. The same furious buzz sounded on the line there. Walk slowly back to the camper. Breathe. Maybe he had reached someone on the east coast. I called my mother in Vermont and my brother on Martha's Vineyard. TVs blared behind their voices. "This means war," my mother said, and then she whispered, "I'm sorry." No word from my son.

The restrained radio announcer's voice went on piling up shocking reports, numbing and incredible. I kept hitting redial, my insides hollowing out. Suddenly, not a buzzing but a ringing sound, followed by his voice. "Hello?"

"Oh, thank God, thank God." Miraculously my call had dropped through a hole in the overloaded satellite network. We spoke briefly. He was walking north through Central Park with his wife, Erinn, and her brother, headed home to his apartment on Ninety-Sixth Street and his three small daughters. Alive and safe. In the midst of the horror coming over the radio a helium balloon of gratitude inflated in my chest.

We headed for town to find a TV. At the campground entrance a staff member stood on the road's shoulder and waved down each car to say, "Turn on your radio." CNN played on the big screen TV in the cavernous Athabasca Hotel bar, and the bartender silently made fresh coffee for us, his only customers. At an Internet café M surfed the wire services. Next to us three young Germans smiled together over their email. In a pizzeria where we choked down lunch the TV played over the heads of inattentive customers. People on the sidewalks went in and out of the hardware store and the bookstore. The air of normalcy in their pace, gestures, and greetings jarred with the swirling fear in my head.

We left Jasper and drove up into the mountains, but there was no solace there. Late afternoon found us back in the Athabasca bar, where a crowd had gathered. The TV was broadcasting live film of explosions in Kabul. Two men in a corner played a video game that flicked multicolored flashes across their avid faces. Otherwise the cocktail hour customers quietly watched the TV. A forty-year-old man dressed like a hard up college student shared our table and began a jumbled commentary on the newscast, more or less directed at me.

"Ain't that just like the US, though? Cowboys."

"Careful, I'm US," I told him.

"Oh, sure, hey, I'm with 'em, I'm American. My mother lives in Greenwich Village, god, I hope she's okay." He retrieved another beer. The TV flickered with images of the president arriving by helicopter back at the White House. "Boy, you'd think they could afford a plane for him," my tablemate slurred. "Where's Air Force One, huh?"

The other occupants of our table, a couple with quiet British accents, glanced over at the tipsy man. "Say," he said to me, "I got a job in New York starting in November. Think I should go?" Why was I talking to this man, anyway?

"Oh, you'll be okay by then." The reassurance could have been meant for either one of us.

"Well, I gotta talk to my mother. She lives on Fifth Avenue, y'know. Right by Rockefeller Center."

The British couple shrugged on their jackets and left. Mark nudged me. "Let's go home." He meant back to the camper.

Canada had become a very cold place. The radio provided streaming news updates, interspersed with talk shows and interviews with Canadian officials. By September twelfth both official and non-official Canadians worried over the airwaves about the US response. An ex-Minister of the Interior spoke slightingly about the American government's ability to remain on high alert for any length of time. At least, it sounded slighting to me. "Just watch us," I yelled at the radio. A woman spoke angrily of the President's talk of defending freedom. "They shouldn't speak as if they have an exclusive right to freedom," she snapped. A man called a talk show host to worry aloud about America's capacity for uncontrolled violence. The host, bless him, responded by saying, "You need to know that right now the anger is incandescent down there. But they do appear to be thinking it out." There were also reports of local vigils for the twin towers victims, of Canadians going to the border in tears to leave behind piles of teddy bears and signs expressing sorrow and sympathy.

I spoke with my son and daughter-in-law daily. I didn't tell them about the Canadian reserve concerning American retaliation. I did tell them about the teddy bears and the sympathy. My son seemed slightly surprised. "It's like being in a foxhole, looking out, Ma. It's good to hear that people elsewhere understand."

I wanted to go home. Home. Or at least back to my country. This northern neighbor nation had become a very lonely place. We packed up and headed south, down the Yellowhead Highway through Avola, Vavenby, Blackpool, Little Fort, Chu Chua, Chinook Cove, McLure and Vinsulla. In Kamloops we picked up the Transcanada Highway briefly and then turned south again on Coquihalla Highway through Hope and Chilliwark. We had decided to cross the border at Sumas, Washington, a pinhead on the map. We reasoned that we had the best chance of avoiding horribly long lines by staying away from the Interstate. The turn for Sumas in Abbotsford, British Columbia was so poorly marked that we almost missed it. We had been riding along past gas stations and fast food outlets yelling at each other about my map reading skills when I spotted the small square sign for Route Eleven South. M swung the rig left in front of a honking phalanx of Canadian cars, and we bounced down through farm country until we sighted a lineup of vehicles parked on the dirt shoulder, engines off, people standing about in the sunshine. Two hours later we were back inside our national borders. It was September sixteenth.

Funny how far from home one could feel in an English speaking country right across one's own borders. Perhaps it's all in the head. One knows oneself to be an alien, so one feels an alien, whether others notice or not. But it's not just that. National character does unite, maybe only because outsiders lump you together. Americans may disagree on so much, but we clash within the confines of a glass bowl that other nations push their noses up against. Humans divide themselves into "us" and "them" in order to organize the overwhelming multitude, from nations, to blocks, to in-laws, to siblings. Draw the line here, see, and stand on this side.

But it wasn't just that invisible geographic barrier stretched across northwestern farmland, punctuated by a scattering of buildings marked Canadian Customs and US Customs, that created my sense of home and not home. While we sat parked on the shoulder, known in Canada as the verge, an eight-year-old boy with shiny blond hair and wide hazel eyes, dressed in red striped t-shirt and cut off shorts, appeared below our windshield, waving up at us. I waved back. "What's it like in there?" he called.

"You want to come in and see?" Before he could mount our top step a younger sister with twin ponytails materialized behind him, then a father, fortyish and sunburned, himself in shorts and t-shirt. An American family, returning from a weekend north of the border, just to get away somewhere and get a little relief, as the dad explained. I didn't ask if they'd had their radio on to local stations during their stay. We didn't talk about it. The lack of personal discussion of the week's events with Canadians, except for my drunken bar companion, had left me standing on the wrong side of an invisible barrier. But here the sense of shared pain was strengthened by our mutual silence on the subject.

More than that in this family let me know that I was closer to home. The boy's forthright approach, the easy laughter of the father in conversation with M, the mother's offhand familiarity and weary protectiveness; it all felt so familiar to me. We had little in common with this family's daily life, so much younger than us and living in a home three thousand miles from ours. But in the warm sunshine of the border they felt like home to me.

I remember a quote from a forgotten source, read long ago, in which an imaginary European says, "Americans! They just smile and smile, and you have no idea what they're thinking." Maybe. This family's impulse to go into Canada for solace, just when I was seeking the comfort of returning home, struck me as passing strange. But I didn't know what the last week had been like for them, bombarded by American media and trying to explain events to their children, while I eked out my news from Canadian radio. We passed a half hour together in superficial exchange, the mother and I chatting about her son's obsession with RVs, M standing in the gravel with the dad. Every so often the men's laughter rang out, unrestrained and free, American.

As the saying goes, home is where, when you have to come there, they have to let you in. The two exhausted customs agents spared their words and never asked what we had purchased in Canada, the routine question earlier in the summer. Only once before had we had a vehicle searched at a border, years ago crossing back from Tijuana to Imperial Beach in California. There I had resentfully raised my trunk lid while a German Shepard sought olfactory evidence of drugs. Here in the loitering warmth of a northern September the female agent entered the RV and inspected the insides, asking about firearms. I threw open cupboards for her. I felt like hugging her. Before we pulled out, M said to the gray faced man, "Thanks for being here." For a second this public employee brightened in his eyes, and he responded, "You travel safe now." The pedestrian exchange brought tears to my eyes. Good grief.

Maudlin or not, it was good to be back on American soil. One night, in a field outside of Lynden, WA, I saw my first plane in the sky since the attack, wheeling up through the darkening twilight, and I stood transfixed and wished it on its way. Everything in my country felt cleaner, brighter, newer, easier, closer.

But I was still adrift. I couldn't relate to the admiring talk about the government administration that I overheard in restaurants, any more than I could stand to contemplate the nascent demonstrations in Seattle demanding that Afghans be protected from the US. We were still three thousand miles from true home. The first of October came and went, and the rent from our tenants had not arrived at my mother's home in Vermont. Maybe they'd lose their jobs, stop paying, have to move out, and we could go home. I hoped for it. Then the rent came. Hope died. M said, "It wouldn't do any good, anyway. Doesn't matter where we are, what we want is to be outside our own skins."

Months later we would visit Ground Zero, listen to the stories of friends and acquaintances who'd been in Manhattan that day, and read the New York Times' measured recounting of lives lost and the families they'd left behind. A year later we would share a table at a wedding with a man who worked near Wall Street and had spent that September eleventh trying to ensure the safety of his employees, while his wife on Long Island wondered if he still lived. His rage burned across the dance music. Two years on I'd sit on my lakefront deck and chat with my high school friend, who has lived for thirty years in lower Manhattan and was still struggling with daily anger and nightly insomnia. M and I had been on the other side of the continent, far away and physically safe. Our injuries were only those of all Americans, insidious and ephemeral. They became part of that year, marking a before and an after.

Nine-eleven knocked the glow out of M's euphoria and emptied out the highways around us. We went on.

9

Not Everything Changes

When wheels support your home, ambivalence shadows your days. You want to go, you want to stay. On any given day, you can do either one. Sounds perfect. It isn't. You spend more time than you want to in planning to go or in struggling to get there. The loss of a reliable hourly structure robbed my days of all the nooks and crannies of time that I was accustomed to count on for my own private pursuits. I alternated between irritability and elation, fatigue and hypomania. At the end of long days of grinding driving, the idea of finding a pretty spot and putting down roots for a week provoked euphoria. But even in the pretty spots, one of us would shortly be at the map, scouting out the next trajectory of our trip and the possibilities for new sights. After all, we were traveling. It's hard work.

Years before we'd taken a guided tour on our first trip to Israel. The lack of any need for making decisions was startlingly relaxing. Somewhere around the second or third day I put words to the floating feeling inside of me: I felt like a happy child. The bus is stopping here, we're getting off, the guide would say. Walk over to this Roman aqueduct, I'll tell you about it. Okay, now be back at the bus in twenty minutes. Today we'll lunch at this falafel stand. Tomorrow we depart the hotel at seven-thirty. The full Israeli breakfast is available to you at six-thirty. When we get to the next hotel, I'll have your room numbers for you. Twenty dollars a person is the customary tip for your driver. Here, I have a bag of persimmons for snacks, help yourself. For a week I tumbled energetically on and off the bus, showed up where I was told to, and otherwise devoted my eyes, ears and thoughts to the wonders of Israel. At the end of the tour, we spent four independent days in Tel Aviv, organizing our own meal schedule and sightseeing. Each evening found us exhausted.

This year in the RV we not only had to set our own itinerary, but we had complete responsibility for all creature comforts, including water (hot or cold,) a working toilet, food for the next meal, heat if needed, etc. After that we could seek entertainment and edification. Want to find out what's interesting in any area? Look for the Visitors' Center, study the map, sort through the clip file accumulated over the past year. Then figure out what's worth seeing and what's not. Save some energy for cooking, cleaning, driving, vehicle servicing, vehicle repair, and getting lost while searching for the grocery store. And don't forget reading and drawing and writing.

This struggle to shape our hours had to be practice for the coming years. We'd stepped off the known path of finding work, establishing credentials, raising children, financing their college, and saving for our own futures. We'd broken the pattern early, on purpose. This wasn't our retirement. This was "a year off," a detour before returning to the well-known mold for a few more years. But I wanted this time to be nothing less than life changing.

Molds break unpredictably. Until they are smashed, one doesn't know where they will split apart, or what the pattern of the remaining pieces will be. Rattling around the continent, adrift on our own impulses, we had no real idea of what shape we'd put our lives into, beyond our vague plans for the next few geographic moves. Our discussions about the future alternated between optimistic dreaming and sharp panic. Were we rendering ourselves unemployable with this gypsy interlude? When the conversation tilted towards fear, one or the other of us would offer reassurance in the form of determined optimism, and the fright would dissipate, fading away to settle back into our last thoughts before sleeping. In the morning we'd travel on.

The idea of home was a panacea for all the difficulties that the days held. Home was where the future would take place. Home became invested with the glow of a solid certainty that when we returned there the new form of our lives would emerge, freshly fashioned out of those shattered pieces. The contours of the next phase would take interesting shape, and we would move forward with an experienced step to embrace our metamorphoses. Balderdash. Life should only hold such simple clarity. But my determined memory of the absolute comforts of home sustained me through the most difficult days of our drifting.

Crossing the US/Canada border into Washington State was a different sort of homecoming, more theoretical in nature. I was back among my countrymen and women. Without the context of nine-eleven, the northwestern state would have felt still quite far from home. Not now. I spent the first week south of the border gazing fondly at the fellow Americans I encountered in supermarkets, restaurants, and campgrounds, imagining our common roots and attitudes. What a wonderful country we shared. The rest of the world could not understand us. We were fellow citizens, united now in danger and battle. We might struggle over tactics and leaders; after all, we were Americans and this was a democracy. In the end we would unite and win the fight together.

Goodness, my patriotism was running high in those weeks. In the coming months, I'd revert to my perennial caution, ferreting out jingoism in flag-waving slogans and participating with discreet listlessness in ubiquitous expressions of nationalistic loyalty like the Pledge of Allegiance at every tourist site. But that was yet to come. That autumn I still glowed with American camaraderie.

It was a rather diffuse, largely unspoken patriotism. M and I continued in the social patterns that had so far marked our trip. We mostly related just to each other. Before starting out, we had developed mutual fantasies about the people we'd be meeting along the way, expanding our friendships to include men and women from all over the country. Go into any RV dealer and you encounter at least one poster photograph of a gathering of about a dozen individuals, all adults over fifty, grouped into a semicircle cemented with smiling eye contact. Often someone holds a guitar in abeyance. They lounge in candy-colored baggy pants and tops, an immensely gleaming RV just behind them, and behind that an orange twilight. Unlike most advertising models, there is no attempt to present these people as examples of fitness or beauty. Some are actually overweight, and hair is either gray or disappearing. Eyeglasses and comfortable footwear adorn the actors. But they look so happy with each other; mouths open in laughter and eyes glinting in shared glances. A slogan may be printed underneath the photo: "Have you met your new friends yet?" Or something like that. Even without the slogan we customers get the point. Buy this fantastically expensive rolling home, and you, too, will be introduced to a society of happy, footloose people and make instant and satisfying friendships wherever you wander.

We never located this community in our travels. We came home no richer in true friends than when we left. We talked to hundreds of people along the way, and I developed new habits for falling into conversation with strangers. But the fact remains: the whole time that we traveled, we never shared a meal with another person that we didn't already know. Looking forward, I would not have predicted this. Looking backward, this fact can make me a little sad. Perhaps we were lacking in some way, or too insular. Perhaps the New England habit of reserve was impossible to break. Raised in that rocky corner of the country, aloofness is a lifelong pattern for me. Until I was ten we lived among fields, my only playmates the two brothers closest to my age. Once in high school, and again a couple of times as an adult, I've been a member of a group. But more often I've moved off alone, or in company with one other person.

Nevertheless, those advertising photos persuaded me that I would break out of my solitary habits and discover the gregarious inner me, striding into the midst of groups with loud and friendly commentary, traveling in bunches to seek entertainment and companionship, returning home with lists of new friends scattered about the country. Hah. Once summer faded and the intensely insular young families disappeared from campgrounds, adults of every age took over. M and I still kept pretty much to ourselves, like every other camper we saw.

It's not true that we never broke bread with any stranger the whole time we traveled. At the beginning of September, in the Canadian Rockies, we pulled the rig in next to a couple about our age from Vancouver. During their sewer line chat Mark told the husband that we planned to visit their home city. An hour later the wife showed up with an invitation for cake and tea after supper, "And we can share some information about Vancouver with you." At eight o'clock we stepped over the pine needles and mounted their steps. Their camper smelled musty. We seated ourselves on brocade-covered chairs. "No, no," the husband said, emerging from the bathroom, "Sit here together on the couch. That way you can both see everything." A foot tall pile of printed material had been laid out on the wood-grained coffee table. We spent the first twenty minutes sharing personal information, in an obligatory exercise of getting to know each other. He was a teacher forced into early retirement by a consolidation in the school system, and happy with this development.

His wife spoke up. "I told him if he was going to retire, I certainly wasn't going to continue working alone." Her voice hinted at a whine. Otherwise, she let her spouse do much of the talking. He described a life style whereby for six months of the year they rented out their house to a couple from Georgia and traveled in their camper.

"They keep it spotless. The fellow fixes everything he finds broken. And the woman gives us free these baskets that she makes and sells." That explained the proliferation of dusty little baskets filled with plastic flowers and tiny stuffed animals scattered around the camper. The man gestured expansively at them, while his wife perched on her dining chair, her face cramped into a tight smile. We tackled the pile of brochures and maps he had readied for us. Forty minutes later we emerged from their camper with a small stack of printed material and a number of ideas as to how to spend our time in Vancouver. Back out on the pine needles, the air smelled clean and sweet. We'd had our first, and as it turned out our last formal invitation to a stranger's camper for the whole trip.

Those advertising pictures at the dealership hung over me less. On my daily walks around campgrounds I never spotted such a group, never had to encounter the adolescent mortification of slipping by unseen on the edges of such a crowd. One afternoon, camped on the Hood Canal in Washington State, I sat and struggled to draw a likeness of the driftwood along the shore, while two guys in the next campsite shot the breeze. These men had fifteen years on us, and their talk was slow, very slow. Of the weather. Campers. Winter plans. Dogs. Canal currents. They talked without force or direction, keeping just enough words suspended in the air to simulate an ongoing conversation while the afternoon passed by. After a while one man's wife joined them and made slighting remarks about the camping abilities of some of their neighbors. No one played a guitar, or told jokes, or even really laughed. I hunched my shoulders over the paper and kept my pencil moving, my back slightly turned. My conscience perched by my ear and whispered, you look unfriendly. I want to be, I replied, I'm busy.

Maybe I never really did want to wander into one of those pictures of happy groups of newfound friends. The only place where I saw anything resembling it was at a large campers' resort in Tucson, where clusters gathered in the dusty dog walks and at the pools, and formed at cocktail time on the cement patios of park model campers. No guitars in evidence. And, of course, throughout the whole state of Florida people seemed intent on conveying their good fortune to each other. Everywhere else across the continent, most socializing with strangers occurred between men who stood about discussing their sewer lines and motor capacities in otherwise deserted campground roads. But, honestly, I'd been of a solitary nature since my rural childhood. Something in me likes it that way. Something else gets sharply lonely, as a result. The road fed both sides of my nature. Moments of lonesomeness for the side that wanted friends occurred regularly, but the solitary one, free in her isolation, thrived on it. There was no social life to maintain.

My only ongoing relationship obligations were to M. If he was lonely, we little discussed it. Married folks move through daily chores with a fairly fixed idea of our spouse's state of mind. But if we pause and try to contemplate the essence of this person who is sharing life's passage with you, marching along through all those swamps, winters, ridges, sultry summers, sudden storms, grinding cold, fog, flashes of sunshine, and failures of forecasts, the question can occur: who is this stranger?

There were times this year that my husband seemed happier to me than he had ever been before. So happy that it knocked me off balance, occasionally annoyed me, and left me uncertain that I still knew him. The grounding depression that hallmarked his disposition disappeared in his disconcerting animation. He sent emails to friends back home and eagerly awaited their replies. He kept a journal. He sought periodic reassurance that I was enjoying myself as much as he was.

M has a natural, outward friendliness to all, but to me he often expresses impatience and boredom with others. Strangers tend to think that he's easy going. His family knows better. He can be intense and critical. He sometimes tells me that no one really has friends, that it's futile to seek them. When we were younger he considered each new couple we met as candidates for the other half of a bonded foursome. It never happened. We had the slightly lopsided friendships that we'd each brought into the relationship, and along the way we met couples to socialize with. Generally one of us liked their counterpart more, and the other partner went along. If the odd person out really disliked their opposite number, the quartet would fade back to a duet that might or might not endure. We each had work colleagues that we took into our confidence. A steady round of parties and gatherings engaged our weekends, invitations generating reciprocations. Such was the pattern of our marital social life before the trip. I'd had my own epiphany that the cure for loneliness was simply the presence of others, intimate or not. M was more of a quality person. Throughout the years, he never really gave up searching for that feeling of intimacy in his friendships and judging them by their failures in this area.

All this we left behind when we hit the road. In our early years together we'd talked of traveling with another couple and discussed possible candidates. By the time we reached the trip, this idea was long dead. There was nobody we could contemplate spending a week in a camper with, let alone a year. We missed home, loved getting emails and were saddened by a blank computer screen. M had his sewer line social scene, but I rarely saw other women, except as they moved between camper and car. On an average walk back in Brookline I used to encounter young mothers stoop sitting, dog owners grouped in the park, and neighbors trudging home from the market. My campground walks outside of Florida and Tucson occurred mostly in a landscape of closed up motor homes with empty picnic tables at their doors. Briefly, in the beginning, I looked for that convivial group with the guitarist. Maybe it's lucky that I didn't find it. I would have been a fish out of water. Better that my capacity to live in lonesomeness strengthen me on the trip. Life was changing and not changing.

10

Grounding

Washington's Olympic Peninsula butts squarely into the Pacific, a place of tall, dark forests shot through with twinkling sunlight and networks of twisting roads. The roads crest hills and drop into earth cuts, curve into the sudden flattening out of a valley and then climb into the woods where it crowds back along the road at the valley's edge. At last reaching the ocean side, we checked in at Mom and Pop's Campground, where Pop did stained glass on the side. The lowering sun shone back across the ocean and lit an oval window six feet across, formed of hundreds of multicolored glass circles set in a vertiginous design that flooded the tumble-down office with rainbow colors.

Every morning I walked the beach, lost in the ephemeral fog that tickles and blankets, conceals and reveals, comforts and deceives all along the continent's edge. My exercise routine had grown to almost two hours a day of walking, biking, weight training, and stretching. I vibrated with well-being. Then suddenly, I dropped into another interlude of unstable hormones. My old friends, irritability, bloat, emotionality, cramps, and fatigue came visiting. For two days I lay about nursing myself. M was a great sport about this, part of his new sunny disposition. When my invalidism had passed we moved eastward to Belfair State Park on the Hood Canal. A sign at the entrance set the rules, including a two-week maximum for any stay, and we decided to remain for the limit. At our campsite on the water's edge we watched the tides from Puget Sound move in and out of the Canal. Each night the moon swelled larger and rose a tiny bit later. One evening loud splashing startled us. The salmon were jumping, multitudes of them in brief glittering flights above their liquid world. Evening after evening this annual instinctive journey entertained us.

It was the last week in September. Yom Kippur was coming. For the first time in years I wouldn't be at the services in our temple back in Massachusetts. I resolved to attend some sort of service for the holiday. Ten years on from declaring myself Jewish by religion, I had a convert's determination. Telephone information connected me with a temple in Tacoma. The young woman on the phone said we could attend the family service without a ticket. On Yom Kippur I dressed in unfamiliar stockings, skirt and pumps, and we drove an hour south to a Tacoma suburb. The anonymous numbered streets were lined with low-slung houses surrounded by stretches of lawn bisected with long concrete driveways. No one walked on the sidewalks, no cars moved along the roads of this depopulated landscape. A mid-century style institutional building appeared on our right. There was no sign, but a wide driveway curved around the building to a mostly empty parking lot behind it. A woman in her early forties swerved her battered Ford Escort past our hesitation, parked her car and strode quickly towards the open doors at the back of the building. Three men wearing yarmulkes stood by the entrance and watched our approach. "L'Shanah Tovah."

Inside the elliptical building wide corridors radiated off from the entrance. A sign directed us to a small side chapel where the family service would be held. Some thirty or forty people had scattered themselves over a few hundred seats by the time the service began. In our temple at home the seats would be jammed for the regular services, but here we had gathered with other strangers in between this temple's membership attended rituals. I stumbled over the unfamiliar prayer melodies. A man rose to speak with the comfortably authoritative air of a temple officer.

"Tonight we must be thankful to find ourselves here together to observe the ancient holiday once again, even as the world around us is caught in terrible crisis." Two nights before someone had come here in the dark to stack fireplace logs against the temple furnace and leave a can of lighter fluid nearby. The pavement of the parking lot had been covered with graffiti that blamed Israel for nine-eleven and demanded the expulsion of all Jews from the country. "Our community went to work to repair the damage with the spirit that is always present here in our temple." And then, the previous night, five hundred neighbors of this temple had showed up after dark, each with a burning candle, encircling the building with a ring of light. The officer's voice cracked slightly as he said, "Our gratitude for their support is immeasurable." Tears stung my own eyes. After the service we left through the same broad doors by which we had entered. No one had questioned or searched us coming in. Just those three men had stood and watched our progress through the parking lot before greeting us with "L'Shanah Tovah." Happy New Year. M replaced his borrowed yarmulke, and we drove home to the camper, to spend the rest of the day reading Torah and the Gates of Repentance prayer book. M fulfilled the commandment to fast; I ate crackers and drank some tea. We rested.

Yom Kippur always scares me. Every year after Rosh Hashanah has passed a slight sense of dread begins gathering in my stomach, building over the eight days between the holidays. Will I be able to endure the long hours of service, the fasting, the review of my past year and its actions? I hope to come out on the other side of the twenty-four hours convinced that something significant has happened. The first few times I marked the day I did feel a transcendence, but in recent years I observe the holiday because it must be observed; that is all and that is enough. This year was my fifteenth Yom Kippur. Fifteen years since we'd joined a temple and started to shape a religious life together, a decade since I'd formally converted from lapsed Protestant to Judaism.

People often change religions because they marry someone of another faith, and the issue of the children's training suddenly seems important. M and I had married in a civil ceremony at City Hall in Manhattan and then nurtured a deep skepticism about all religions in our sons as they grew up. My conversion was an act of determination on my own part and for my own sake. By the time I decided to do it, I thought I was beyond seeking approval or fearing censure from anyone. Still, when my father-in-law initially responded by saying, "That doesn't make you Jewish," I had cried angry tears. I retorted to M, "I still don't like Jewish food." To my knowledge, no one repeated my remark to my mother-in-law. Months later my father-in-law and I would sit in the pale yellow living room of his south Florida condo and discuss the thinking that had brought me to my decision. This tough old man, committed to socialism since his youth, had no use for religious belief of any kind, but that day he offered grudging acknowledgement of my sincerity. Later the four of us toured Lion Country, an hour west of their home, and he gazed out the car window and gave a soliloquy about the immense beasts' life cycle, ending by declaring, "And they accomplish it all without God." As I say, he was tough.

Conversion lands a person in a permanent no man's land. Mine rendered me mysteriously Jewish to my family and gentile friends, a source of answers for their cautious questions about pork and Hanukah. Jewish colleagues and friends responded with mixtures of pride and suspicion. My rabbi danced with happiness when I told him of my decision. A male friend shook my hand and said, "Welcome to the tribe," and thereafter never missed an opportunity to speak scornfully of Jewish ritual. Another old friend, member of a conservative temple and reasonably observant, scowled at me in surprise and asked, "What for?" When I ventured that I wanted a spiritual experience, she went off into gales of laughter.

My conversion came as I approached fifty years old. Those who convert to another religion at a younger age may more fully cloak themselves in the identity of the new group. My alteration of religious loyalty rendered me always some-what of an outsider in matters of community and shared faith. There it was again, that theme of being the loner, the outlander. It wasn't altogether an uncomfort-able position, once the initial glow of the conversion wore off. Anyway, I had an official faith, something I'd lacked since adolescence. My kids, who had absorbed well my previous lessons on doubting all religious maxims, registered alarm and worried aloud that I might take this whole thing too far. Their attitude reflected my efforts to inculcate agnosticism in them, but I'd changed my own mind, somewhere in my forties. I told them that I wanted a structure to hang my spiri-tual hat on, a connection with a group of people thinking about moral dilemmas. Okay, Ma, just don't get carried away.

Converting is thrilling, an emotional high. It's better than falling in love because it's calmer; it doesn't rest precariously on one other human being but rather envelops one with the warm haze of a whole new community. The eupho-ria brought on by a conscious redefinition of priorities lasts for a while. I was con-fident that by declaring my new status I had accomplished what I set out to do. I had reordered my perception of the world within a structure hammered out by Jews over five millennia. The new order cleared my view along the line of life's perspective, I was sure.

My sons might worry that their mother would begin to eschew the light switches on Shabbat, keep separate sets of dishes, and maybe even take to wearing a wig. M, also, reacted to my change. Raised by his father to believe in socialism if in anything, bar mitzvah at thirteen largely because his friends were doing so, a participant with me in raising our children to view organized religion as probably delusional, he responded to my initial middle-aged religious gropings with an intense period of Kabalistic study and a sudden determination to follow all mitz-vot. Since there are 613 of these in the Torah, for practicality he needed to restrict his focus somewhat. For a while he insisted on not carrying money on Shabbat, and he watched closely for correct procedure when I performed the blessings on Friday nights. The lack of religious training for our sons now trou-bled him. He seemed to hope for my epiphany to be contagious and voiced dis-appointment in their failure to show allegiance to Judaism.

Time takes away the novelty and thrill of any new thing. All religions have clay feet, and the toes of mine began to poke out after a couple of years. My embracement of committee work at our temple led to requests for more involve-ment, until I grew tired and resentful. The constant fund raising necessary to sus-tain the place began to irritate. The faint but unremitting drumbeat of a worry about whether we were observant enough provoked me to impatience. My own childhood religious training had been very low Protestant, with an emphasis on rigorous examination of the moral consequences of one's actions and little importance afforded to ritual. Such a background predisposed me to a determination to exercise some freedom of choice in how I observed my new religion. By no coincidence, that religion was Reform Judaism, not Orthodox or Conservative. Within the sometimes-quarrelsome Reform community I seemed to find what I was looking for: a suggested structure around which to arrange my world perception and a set of standards to try to adhere to. If the Judaic creed seems flinty and difficult, if my adherence to it frequently reminds me of my alien antecedents, well, such attributes harmonize with other life patterns I've developed. At the end of Yom Kippur, 2001, when the sun had sunk into gold and rose washes over the canal water, we ate a steak dinner and began to talk about what would come next.

Late September was delivering beautiful weather, and for a few days we'd avoided the news on TV and the radio in a selfish wish for some personal peace. Twice we'd taken the ferry into Seattle to spend time with my stepson, who lived there. He was deeply into the nascent protest movement against US government responses to the terrorism. The three of us trailed up and down the hills of that seedy, pretty city, two men in intense conversation about politics, and one woman drifting ahead and behind them, gorging her senses on the shop windows, restaurant odors, and pedestrian conversations of this northwestern American outpost. By some quirk of luck good weather seems to join me in Seattle whenever I visit, which must be one reason why I hold the place in such high regard. The last day there the three of us walked miles, beginning at the northern tip of the Pike's Place area and rambling through the Seattle Center area and on to the University neighborhood, where we feasted on spicy meat wrapped in sour bread at a North African restaurant. Then stepson and I lost ourselves in one of his favorite used book stores for an hour or so. It was a day of love, of sharing, of enjoyment and appreciation for each other. It was time to part, before any of us blew it. He got back into his rattletrap car to drive home, and we returned to the ferry terminal to board one of those muscular boats that carry commuters and their fellow travelers about Puget Sound. Fog and dark came down on us by the time we docked in Belfair. With October just ahead, our short-term goal was a couple of leisurely weeks exploring the Oregon coast, then a return east in November for an extended family visit.

Siuslaw River in Florence, Oregon

11

The State Of Oregon

Oregon's pale golden beaches roll unimpeded next to US 101, their sandy undulations and the repetitive diagonal sweep of surf at their edges drawing the cruising car and its entranced occupants on for miles. My first oceanic memories are of the edgy Maine coast, where sharp promontories divide and challenge the chaotic surf. The roads there writhe next to the ocean, twisting inland away from the views of huge aquatic undulations, to spin about on the turn of a precipice and drop the traveler in front of another white water display. In Oregon we drifted south for a whole morning without ever losing sight of the Pacific. The deceptively gentler nature of the left coast was echoed in the forty-foot tall trees and the thick vegetation spilling over the sandy hills. The daily fog that seeped across the land from western waters whispered a climatic echo of New England's pulverizing storms. Standing on this shoreline, face turned into the steady, gentle wind, the meaning of the Pacific Rim came to me. Only the imagined shores of China, Japan, and Vietnam could make that expanse of restless water seem vaster and more exotic than the huge grey ocean in my childhood's backyard. Here I walked from the forested confines of our campground out past curving stands of sea grass to open rolling dunes, then turned south and hiked on uninhibited, as far as I chose to go. Growing up in Maine, I had become used to the confines and dangers of rocky inlets. Here I could shed my shoes and spread my toes in the sand, stepping through the miles until only my own fatigue turned me back to the beginning. The freedom of it intoxicated my daily exercise routine.

Our real freedom was becoming sharply curtailed by snowballing vehicle problems. We'd been lucky so far, crossing a continent with our two motorized contraptions and encountering little difficulty with their mechanical operations. This luck couldn't last. Trouble had first glimmered coming south on the Yellowhead Highway out of the Canadian Rockies, when we'd begun to lose a tire on the car. Rolling down through that immense landscape that dwarfed the tandem tractor-trailers who shared the road with us, we had to stop every fifty miles and pump air back into the errant wheel. New tires in Seattle corrected the problem. Three weeks later the car's transmission suddenly restricted us to second gear. We got that fixed in Portland. Back out on the coast, the automatic alarm on the car went crazy right in the middle of Florence, a pretty tourist and fishing town on the Siuslaw River. After munching fried oysters while gazing out over moored fishing boats and the river's arching bridge, we had returned to our car and set off a wailing screech that rattled the whole town. The only way to stop it was to relock the car while standing beside it on the sidewalk. This wouldn't do. M called the manufacturer's eight hundred number and reached someone in the mid south, for whom we might as well have been on the other side of the moon. This person had no idea how to disable the alarm. "They're built that way, for security, you know, sir." He suggested a dealer in Portland, a hundred and seventy miles away. But a friendly young woman in the nearby gift shop told us her mother had bought a car from a dealer in Corvallis, ninety miles closer. Ninety miles less on the towing bill made a big difference. Off the car went, chained to a flat bed trailer, fully functional except for the alarm that denied all access to its rightful owners. Let's leave nameless the manufacturer and their brainless designers

Travel can present an onerous problem and then suddenly reward you with an unexpected delight. Corvallis is a pretty college town, and it was full of October sunshine and the zest of a young fall semester when we were there. In fact, we were there, and there, and there again. Three times the dealer fixed the alarm; three times we returned to the coast; three times the alarm wailed again, miles from the mechanic. The second and third times we towed it back ourselves behind the RV, rather than re-engaging the dearly priced flat bed truck. Our last afternoon on the Oregon coast we walked the curving hills at Oregon Dunes National Recreation Area, pounding sand and deciding it was time to buy a new car. Three thousand miles from home we needed to dump this buggy and dicker with a car salesman. So much for the hypnotic leisure of the coast.

Back to Corvallis we went, the autumn sun still warm and sweet, the campground we'd been frequenting still open east of town. I was getting to know the owner's preference in TV news (Fox, not CNN,) and her opinion of the high school basketball team (sure fire winners, good boys all, not a prima donna in the bunch.) One evening she insisted on going to her own kitchen for a loaf of bread when I asked for a nearby store, and none were open. In town we grabbed meals at a coffee house filled with orangey butcher block tables, a chalkboard with soup and bagel specials scrawled on it, a rack of newspapers hanging in slanting sunshine, and two pretty blonds behind the counter. Beyond its plate glass front the wide sidewalks of a six-block-deep downtown area still enjoyed the shade of tall deciduous trees. Pedestrians in jeans or lightweight business clothing strolled past eighty-year-old mottled brick buildings, elderly by western standards. In one such structure, which had been converted from its previous unilateral use to an indoor warren of artists' shops, I found handmade pendant earrings with turquoise, jade, copper and burgundy colored stones for ten dollars each. The woman with flowing gray hair who sold them to me chatted about the artist's preference in stones. Back out on the street people smiled and nodded. "Good morning." "How y'all doing today?"

Just north of this petite urban oasis the sidewalks petered out where the strip malls and gas stations of a less picturesque American commercialism lined the road. A cluster of car dealerships displayed their shining commodities in neat lines that snaked across contiguous parking lots. Bolstered by the warmth of this collegiate western town, we chose a brand competitive to the one with the wailing alarm and strode into the showroom, where half a dozen cold-faced salesmen gazed into the space just beyond their glass cubicles. One stood and approached. "Hi, folks, I'm Phil, can I be of assistance to you?" he asked with the friendly animation appropriate to his task. Thus began three days of the detailed struggle required in order to drive a new car away from their parking lot.

Trading cars out of state is a cumbersome process, when the title of the one you own is locked in a safe deposit box thousands of miles away, when your insurance agent is three time zones away, and when your salesman assumes you have a helpful relationship with the motor vehicle registry from hell that inhabits your native state. Long stretches of down time sitting idly by Phil's desk were broken by brief interludes when he returned to report the dealer's side of negotiations or, later, to suggest paperwork strategies acceptable to the business office. No other customers disturbed the peace of the showroom. Three other salesmen sat at their desks gazing into the air, taking and making phone calls, rising to walk slowly to the double glass doors and back. Not once did one even nod in our direction. After one six-hour stint by Phil's desk, we returned the next afternoon to find his chair empty. I stood directly before the desk next door and inquired as to Phil's whereabouts. Phil's colleague turned his reluctant gaze on me, eyes as blank as if he'd never seen me and barely heard of the gentleman that I inquired after. He stated that he had no information as to the fellow's whereabouts and went back to examining empty space, conveying that he also had no inclination to find out.

Phil showed up on his own shortly thereafter, and M and I whiled away another day in plastic chairs, wondering whether the salesmen all hated each other, or hated ours in particular, or had orders from the boss not to poach on each other's customers, or were deeply depressed by the post nine-eleven lack of business, or had picked up our eastern accents and hated pushy Yankee Jews. One doesn't seek the ambience of a small artists' store within the expanse of polished linoleum of a car agency. But this place had achieved new levels of coldness in the world of commercialism. The afternoon of the third day we drove our new white sedan off the lot and forgot about those stone-faced men.

Our enthusiasm for returning to the coast had waned. Let's go home, we said to each other, we're due there next month anyway, let's skip flying and hike east by car and RV. It was this kind of impulsive turn in direction that lofted our spirits throughout the year. But wait; let's stop by Las Vegas first. No, it wasn't logical: look at the map. It was impulsive and insane. All the more reason to do it. We laughed and headed north up Interstate 5, to pick up Interstate 84 and head east through the Columbia River Gorge.

Some giant builder of sand castles has designed the Gorge in heroic proportions and magical atmospheres. Light sculpts deep concavities in the huge hills on the south side and flattens the contours on the north side into two-dimensional soaring curves. At the nadir rolls the glittering river, swerving about within its valley confines but ever headed west in its sinuous drive to the sea. Melodrama as landscape. So what possessed me to be knitting while we drove through this heroic valley? Because that's what I was doing, counting out cables in two, four, two, three, two, four, two, six rhythm, glancing up through the window and down again to my lap. We were traveling east on the shadowed southern bank where the road rhythmically climbed and dipped through the sweeping hills, ever in view of the navy blue river and the northern banks, which rose like the pale dun flanks of an enormous deer against the ultramarine sky. I played a game with myself: how long could I gaze at this beauty and keep my knitting fingers going until I was forced to look back down at the wool? Thus I took in this colossal river basin in segments only. Perhaps that is sad. Perhaps the sweeping wholeness of that place was overwhelming.

Perhaps the idle hours at the car dealership drove the insistent click of the knitting needles. Accomplishment gives meaning and worth to one's days and weeks. Go without it and depression sets in. This possibility panics me into activity, any activity. It must be the result of growing up with a depressive father. I would creep by his study on dark afternoons to see him stretched out in passive agony, or watch as he joylessly chewed his supper food, longing to rescue him from the despairing abyss.

Fifty years on, I feared the inheritance of his anguished idleness. I had to keep busy, produce, work. For decades, my jobs created a sense of industry. Now something else must substitute: knitting, drawing, something. Housekeeping and sightseeing weren't enough. But these insights weren't clear to me in the Columbia River Gorge. I just kept up my frantic double tracked activity of twisting blue gray wool into the cabled pattern and drinking in the landscape. When we halted for the night at The Dalles, in a truck stop campground by the shadow of the Route 197 Bridge, I'd added six inches to the sweater sleeve.

Another day of driving and then goodbye to Oregon. We'd seen too little and too much of it. We'd met great people when our car broke down: the girl who helped us find a dealer, the man who offered us a ride back to our camper and then waited forty-five minutes to perform his favor while M dealt with the tow truck. The transmission shop in Portland. I cannot leave the Oregon chapter without telling of the transmission shop in Portland. With our car operating on second gear only we had crept into Aamco on McGillivray Boulevard, ready for the worst of news. While M discussed our problems with the shop manager, I examined the testimonial cards from happy customers that were tacked to a dusty bulletin board. Hah! I thought. How old are these things? The edges of some of them curled up in age. Did the shop really think that anybody believed them? We rented a car and went out to explore the city that we hadn't planned to come to, while we awaited expensive news.

Portland turned out to be a pretty nice town. Our campground lay along the Willamette River, where hundreds of houseboats crowded nearby piers, ranging in style from modern to Victorian and from basic boxes to multistoried, balconied structures. A high school friend of our son showed us around the Northwest neighborhood and took us on a walk into the backside of Washington Park at dusk, up a rough path through funky woods, with her two mongrels and her boy friend as companions. She is an artist and had won a commission a year previously to enter a design in Seattle's display of pig statuary throughout the city. Her clever concoction to mock capitalism was of a hog with hind legs formed of the twin towers. Now, showing us photos of the sculpture created in a different era, embarrassment flattened her eyelids and drew down the corners of her mouth, where a tiny diamond-like stud glittered. We took her and her good looking boyfriend from Texas to the Tuscan Grill on Twenty-Third Street, where their enthusiasm for their dinners sharpened my appreciation of my own fennel salad and grilled rabbit. In her articulate way, she described their journey west from New York and their process in choosing Portland for their next home. I liked this young couple a lot, so consciously shaping their lives.

The best part of Portland was the call that came from the transmission shop the next day while we were wandering about the Japanese Garden in Forest Park. The car repair bill totaled seventy-eight dollars. One small part had failed, not the whole transmission. And yes, I wrote them a testimonial. Two hobbled out-of-towners had come into their shop. They could have sold us practically anything, including a new transmission. That yellowing bulletin board had told the truth.

Our last day in the state we shadowed the Oregon Trail, traveling in the opposite direction from the pioneers, and camped at Farewell Bend State Park in Huntington, paying fifteen dollars for a spot along waters tangential to the Snake River. At the local truck stop I sought to rent a video. An Indian family of a mother and three half grown children watched me silently with agitated fear in their eyes. A young white man with sinewy arms sat in a chair by the door, glowering at me. No one spoke. The place had no videos, and I walked out silently, feeling too rich in my shorts and t-shirt. A new moon slipped beneath the western horizon, while the fading red sunset simultaneously withdrew color from the soft tan banks of the river. We ate supper listening to David McCullough's biography of John Adams on the tape deck. In the morning we'd arise at dawn to cross into Idaho for another long driving day.

12

Going Home

The whole country had put up signs: "Thanks for traveling." Motels' marquees, hand lettered boards at gas stations and restaurants, and billboards scattered across the yawning western reaches all conveyed mixed messages of belligerence and grief. "Remember the fallen." "God bless NYC." "God bless the USA." "Osama, the check is in the mail." "These colors don't run." "United We Stand."

The long stretches of empty Interstate in southern Idaho held only the green and white official signs that marked exits for single ranches. The occasional vehicles passing us made up for this lack of stationary messages with bumper stickers: "We will never forget." "Remember the Pentagon." "Lock and load." Patriotism shimmered on the airwaves. While radio talk shows chattered with rage, traffic thinned to nothing on the pavement running past desiccated hills that humped upward into the blue mountains of Idaho. Scattered clusters of yellowing trees stood against their huge indigo sides. By Utah we were frequently alone on the road. Is it always this empty out here, or is this a sign of the times?

We rolled past the huge RV paradises crowding against the highway in St. George, Utah and on through the sudden abutments of the Virgin Mountains in Arizona's northwestern corner. Las Vegas had scaled its signs thanking travelers to its own fantastic reality. Hotels rooms were dirt-cheap. We checked into a suite with a double Jacuzzi at Circus Circus for sixty-five dollars. Crowds mobbed the casino, flowed around the clown displays and formed a looping registration line. The cabdriver who carried us down the Strip insisted that business was way down. "I'm sure the tourists will come back soon. Not worried about it at all," he declared as we gazed out the window at the hordes flocking along the sidewalks. What's it like in this town when it's busy, I wondered. Last time we'd visited Vegas, in 1979, it was equal parts seedy and slick. In twenty-two years it had exploded in size and pretentiousness. We squeezed in among the sidewalk throngs to watch pirates vanquish pompous Englishmen, and waterfalls reflect rainbows. My favorite free show was the implosion of the Desert Inn at two AM on our last night. The old casino gave three loud cracks and then collapsed in a crumbling wave that started at the ground and rose upward, bringing down the roofline in a sudden sweep from right to left.

We headed east towards Georgia, planning to store the RV there before going north for November. Outside of Memphis one Saturday morning bolts fell out of the car hitch, and the car started ramming the RV every time we braked. I stood on the shoulder and stared down early truck traffic while M dismantled the crippled towing mechanism, and we finished the trip to Savannah with two drivers. There we'd get it fixed, and wait for the next vehicle problem to arise. None did, for the rest of the year. Other hurdles took their place.

Northward we went. In New England, the bare trees and brown fields, the sting of cold air in the nostrils and the weight of wool against my skin strengthened my Yankee guts for the second half of the year. The company of friends and family nurtured. With the freedom of the unemployed homeless, we moved about in serial visits, from Boston, to Martha's Vineyard, to Stowe, Vermont, Poughkeepsie, New York, and finally to our son's home in Manhattan.

The last night in New York I awoke at five AM in his apartment on East Ninety-sixth Street and wondered sleepily why my daughter-in-law was lighting candles at that hour. Suddenly Erinn was screaming, "Get the baby!" her feet pounding away down the long hallway towards the old maid's room in back of the kitchen. Gray smoke already obscured the hallway floor. Crouch down, stay low. In my son's bedroom two sleepy granddaughters raised their heads at the foot of the bed. I grabbed the oldest one and crab walked to the apartment door, only to stand helpless before its stack of locks. Remember to put your palm flat against the door. Okay, it's cool, we can go out. Except for those locks: two deadbolts, a chain, a shafted police lock. The whole array began to disappear behind smoke swirls just as my son's hand brushed past me and flicked knobs. We all tumbled down the stairs and out onto gritty concrete, barefoot in our pajamas. The three-year-old in my arms had begun to scream for her mother. A man pushed past us and ran into the building, yelling "Fire! Fire!" Other people milled about, some holding children. Erinn and I wordlessly exchanged children, and her seven-month-old snuggled into my arms. For the next three hours I hugged this quiescent bundle, first on the sidewalk, then up in the apartment of friends next door. I sat in a rocker and fed the baby the bottle I was handed, ostensibly helping, but knowing that it was only her warm weight against my chest that stopped the shaking in my own body. She and I swayed back and forth in the rocking chair and watched the hubbub about us: she dozing from time to time, me wrapped in a blanket, as people raced by, the friends got ready for work, the phone went from hand to hand, and my son passed occasionally, gray-faced and distracted.

The sense of our good luck came on almost immediately. After all, the fire had started in the deli just below the apartment and accelerated up the airshaft to destroy all the apartments on the floor directly above it in minutes. The smoke alarms in the apartment had never sounded. We had all been asleep at the time. My son was scheduled to leave on a business trip later that day: twenty-four hours later his wife would have been alone in the apartment with three children under the age of four. Feeling lucky is part of being in shock. Disbelief and reflexive fear come later, but initially the mind races off on adrenaline rides. Above my rocking head high-spirited conversations about new furniture punctuated discussions about emergency housing. My son moved from sidewalk check-ins with the firemen to consultations in the friends' apartment with such speed that he almost achieved a presence in two places at once. I lost track of M for long minutes, and then he would reappear, talking about the landlord or the insurance company. At one point he suddenly stood before me with an egg sandwich, which I gobbled up. The two older grandchildren raced about in frantic play, mirroring the adults' hysteria. My own mind and body hunkered down behind the barricade of the sleeping baby, quietly watching the melee around me. Later that day M and I left the city and headed south, making it all the way to Delaware before stopping, enveloped in giddiness, our skin reeking of smoke, hungry to the point of dizziness before we thought to do anything about it. We found a buffet restaurant and attacked the cooling food, then checked into a motel, giggly and spinning. Two months later an extra fumigation charge for the room showed up on our credit card. We paid it. We really did stink.

We rolled southward, the weather warming, the days slightly longer, the rest of the year ahead of us. First there would be the Florida Keys, then west again. The RV awaited us in the backfield of a campground outside of Savannah. Climbing into it provoked a happy sense of homecoming. In Las Vegas we'd seen the Cirque de Soleil show, "O", in which the water depth had appeared to change, one minute allowing for acrobats to high dive off of forty foot boards, another minute supporting a damsel who tiptoed ankle deep across the stage. My own mentality mirrored this shifting depth, one minute seeking the meaning of my life, at another minute engrossed in the pretty pictures in a decorating magazine.

The neighbors' lobby provided refuge from the fire:
me, Gracie, Katie, Ryan and Chris

13

Southern Views

Florida holds few charms for me. The state enchants M, embodying his memories of summers before adolescence, when he would spend three anticipatory June days in the backseat of the family car, growing sweatier every hour, watching the shoulders of Route 1 move by, a decade before the Interstates began introducing their efficient speed to American travelers. At the end of their journey his mother's parents awaited them in South Miami Beach before it was hip, when it was still a place of bungalows and cheap delis. His grandparents had left Polish Corridor frigidity to labor for decades in America and finally reward themselves with a retirement four blocks from the southern ocean, where they spent their days dressed neck to heels in the modest garb of their youth. M's dour father, released from his double jobs back in New York, donned a swimsuit to play with his children in the surf and buy them afternoon sweets along Collins Avenue. Of course the whole state glows for M. All I can see is the abiding flatness, relieved only by thirty-storied condos that blot out ocean views, sun rotted strip malls, and the stick straight roads leading into the muggy, buggy interior. I've never taken to Florida, and it's never taken to me.

Except for the Keys. This is the only place in the state where I approach M's enthusiasm. After picking up the RV in Georgia we headed straight south to spend three weeks on this rocky island chain, working our way down through Marathon Key, Bahia Honda State Park, and finally to Key West. Here our campsite backed onto a bay across from the Naval Air Station, and the wind blew for ten straight days and nights off the turquoise water. Fighter planes crashed through the sound barrier in morning exercises, frigate birds sliced the air closer in, and two helicopters hovered over Zachary Taylor State Park at twilight on the night that I saw that storied exit of the sun over the southern sea, the green flash. I kept my determined gaze on the sinking red ball until a steady emerald glow spread across the horizon line. A mental flash immediately informed me that the visual effect occurs within one's own eyes, like gazing at a red square and then watching the square reappear in green on a blank white page. The heavens surely have nothing to do with it. (Three years later an astronomer would disabuse my egocentricity in his explanation of refraction and the colors of the sun.)

We rode our bikes past palmetto groves and concrete abutments into downtown Key West to eat at Duval Street restaurants with names like Crabby Dick's. We biked back past a cemetery of four-story crypts, slowly crumbling to earth on a sultry side street. Sexual sightseeing was ubiquitous. Young bodies of both genders paraded all but nude on streets and beaches. We ogled. I grew sad with the disappointment over our own aging bodies. M just kept looking.

One day we took the tour to Fort Jefferson, forty miles out across the water. For three hours I flattened my tongue on the floor of my mouth to avoid biting it off while the boat slammed over ocean swells. Finally the pilot cut the howling engines, and we drifted in beside a huge hexagonal brick structure floating in the middle of turquoise water. In the enchanted atmosphere created by the ruddy brick, azure sea and brilliant green vegetation, the guide recounted a history crowded with disease, starvation and madness in this watery prison. Then while M snorkeled, I went back inside alone and walked the receding arches of the inner walls, wondering about the ghost stories piled in their corners. No apparition appeared, but the boat blasted its cracked whistle call to re-board, and I joined a dripping M. We headed back by speed boat across the same water over which seven slaves had fled in a canoe during the fort's construction in the early eighteen hundreds. When they were caught, they dove into the warm water to try to drown themselves. But manpower like that was valuable, and their captors managed to save them from the sharks and return them to their bondage. I watched the cobalt water undulate past our returning boat and thought of those lives worse than death, while M repacked his snorkeling gear and spoke of lovely colored fish. He saw pretty bodies and iridescent fish, and I was compelled to brood on loss and sadness. Too long a social worker, perhaps.

Time to leave the Keys. The prices we were paying for everything couldn't be sustained by our budget, and this, not our irremediable differences on Florida, drove us back north again. We didn't discuss these differences; I just felt the weight of them. M's jubilation with life, muted by nine-eleven, returned to set my teeth on edge at certain moments. But how do you say to your spouse, "Your bloody happiness is sending me around the bend," without sounding small minded? I was feeling pretty happy these days, but I couldn't match his elation at finding himself in an RV for a year of freedom, and in Florida to top it off. We gave up our seventy-eight dollars a night camping spot and headed back up

Route A1A to Homestead, home base for a week of visiting friends and relatives in greater Miami.

Days flowed by. On return from our Thanksgiving trip north I'd completely converted over to paper dishes and sworn off all complicated cooking. My idea of RV interior decoration had evolved to one of clean, bare surfaces. Exercising in the balmy subtropical air was seductively easy, and I'd continued to lose weight, ten slow pounds since starting the trip. It's hard to sustain irritability about anything when the number on the scale keeps creeping downward. The Keys had been on M's 'must do' list for the year, and we'd done them thoroughly, until even he was ready to leave. All in all, a very satisfactory view of things bounced back and forth between the two of us.

I awoke contented on the last day of the year. We'd made plans to visit Hammocks Park for a bike ride and then attend the campground's New Year's Eve party. At least I think it was Hammocks Park. One day, while searching for a relative's home in southwest Miami, we had found a lovely place where waxy white pendant blooms hung among leathery leaves in shades of olive and maroon, and shaded trails ran beside the quiet water of meandering streams. We decided to return with our bikes the next day. It might have been Hammocks. I hope I get to go there again someday.

Fort Jefferson, Dry Tortugas National Park, Florida

14

Loss

At nine-thirty AM the cell phone jingled its electronic bell, and Mark answered. My younger brother on the Vineyard was calling to report that Mom had had a "small stroke." This was the same brother who had remarked over the phone to me on nine-eleven, "I really need to turn the TV off and get back to work here." He can't be called an alarmist and surely doesn't like to be diverted from his labor. He was now saying to me on the phone, "At ninety-three, I'm not sure there is such a thing as a small stroke. I'm just getting a space on a ferry boat, I'm going to go up to Vermont to see what's going on." I started packing.

She died at two-thirty that afternoon. She spent the last five hours of her life lying in a bed in the local hospital, without tubes or wires, in her own nightgown. Her second son sat by her side, and shortly after lunchtime he agreed to have a little morphine administered, when the nurse suggested that her twitching might be indicative of pain. Earlier, while she still lay in the emergency room, my older brother had called me and held the phone receiver to her ear. I screamed down the line, "I love you. You are an inspiration to me, for the rest of my life. I love you and Mark loves you. We're coming, hold on, we're on our way." Probably the nicest thing I ever said to her. She didn't wait after hearing that, and I choose to believe that she did hear it. Four hours later she let go of her long, complicated life, happiest in the last years, and slipped past us and away.

My brother called to tell me as we were driving up Don Shula Expressway towards Miami International Airport. I wept. I sobbed and screamed. I pounded my feet on the car floor until I thought I might punch a hole in the metal. M's face glistened, but he kept the car on the road. I could not have done that. I couldn't do anything but shuffle along behind while he checked us into an empty motel, made phone calls, got pizza, arranged a cab for the morning, talked to our sons, and put me to bed.

New Year's Day the airport was crowded. People stood in line wearing cardboard hats with 2002 emblazoned on them in neon colors. A family waited in front of us with two young children, three trolleys of baggage, and a boxer dog in a cage. A bride and groom, still dressed like cake decorations and surrounded by friends, swooned and giggled in a corner. We were singled out and searched and x-rayed each step of the way. Buying tickets the day before with an open-ended return had set off every post nine-eleven bell in the airline computers. Courteous airline staff kept approaching us to pull us out of lines, asking us to step aside to where they could open and examine our suitcases, frisk us, question us, and delay us. Always politely explaining this was just routine and completely random. It didn't matter. I moved numbly through it all. Place my body here, open this bag, stand over there, listen to M explain again that his mother-in-law had just died. Let the minutes keep moving forward. Nothing really mattered, except the endless slide of memory inside my head.

Mom's last house, Hyde Park, Vermont

15

War

We had fought so much through the years. I didn't believe that I was a difficult child, but being the only girl in four children made me hers in a way that her sons weren't. "I wanted a girl so badly," she always said, shining at me. That statement always curdled my stomach juices a little. Our separation when I was thirteen and went off to boarding school had opened yawning difficulties between us. She was the one who decided that I should leave home, not me and not my father. My brothers stayed in the local high school, but I went off to a private school education. This southern California girl who had dreamed of attending Wellesley was determined that her daughter would know a wider world beyond the small New England town where my parents had finally settled after the transcontinental wanderings of the first decades of their marriage. She realized her ambition for me and reaped the rewards of the antique warning: be careful what you wish for. Off I went to meet the children of families from Boston, Connecticut and New York, the offspring of South American diplomats, and the occasional heir of a clan from Utah or Ohio. Off I went to hear stories of other families' lives and the expectations for their futures from girls who looked a lot like me, but were allowed to use makeup already. Mom stayed home with her dreams for me and for herself. Each year of the four I spent at boarding school I stepped further away from those dreams, grew more hostile to my parents' expectations for my future, and claimed more independence of thought.

Fifty miles separated my family's home in southern Vermont and the all girls' school on rolling hills just east of the Connecticut River in Massachusetts' Hampshire County. The punctuation of three short vacations during the academic year and two months at home in the summer highlighted the extent to which I was changing, slipping out of my own clan's culture, and challenging my parents with new ideas that I hadn't learned at the parental dinner table. For the first two years homesickness pulverized me every time I returned to school. By the time I was a junior it had receded, and I turned my resentment at being exiled from daily family life into a constant challenge to Mom and Dad's way of thinking. I would never live at home full time again. This was not what my mother had bargained for. My father mostly kept his own silent counsel.

My mother had done most of the hands-on child rearing in our family, while my father remained a shadowy figure, conducting his own intense relationship with her in the wings of the stage on which she organized the plots of our days and instructed our characters. With my departure to boarding school, she was the one who led the home base effort to retain family influence over my mind and heart. I fought back with the fury of a teenage girl ousted too early from the insularity of family life and daily absorbing her classmates' tales of wider worlds. Pitch battles ensued. Our escalating contests of crying, screaming, and hurt feelings rent the air during junior and senior year vacations. Nothing ever really got resolved. My two brothers who still lived at home went off to their local social lives and kept their opinions to themselves. My father stayed in his study and left the lights off.

I fell in love with New York City by proxy, through the stories of my more sophisticated classmates. Constant begging extracted two trips there with my parents by the time I graduated. The summer between high school and college I worked my first job away from home, at a lake resort in mid-state Vermont, and linked up with a boy from the city. With the force of a determination I was hardly conscious of, I went forward to marry three years later and land myself in New York full time.

I wonder if my parents really thought that after the years of education and friendships away from home, I would docilely return to their small town, find a local boy to marry and live down the street. Maybe they did. After all, they had both lived with their own parents until marrying. They had the grace to throw us a big wedding, but the conflicts weren't over. Overwrought phone conversations, long and emotional letters, ultimatums concerning holiday plans, and periods of not speaking to each other continued between my mother and myself. Occasionally she reported her version of my father's opinions. Inside their rambling colonial, he stuck to his study's gloom, sitting quietly with a glass in hand. At age sixty-seven, when I had just turned twenty-six and my son was two months old, he took himself completely out of the fray by dying. Two months after that my husband walked out of our apartment in Brooklyn and found someplace else to live.

My mother and I were left alone in the fight, without buffers or allies, just the two of us. Well, not just two. My infant son had entered the scene. His ten-pound existence lent force to my mother's determination that I return to live near her, protected and supported by her in my new role as single mother. The idea of submitting to her will at all, something I'd already fought against for a decade, terrified me. Her own raw bereavement and my confused grief over my melting marriage lent propellant fuel to our firefights. Things got worse.

Things got ugly. I squirm at the memory of what we said to each other. She went for the vulnerable underbelly, and so did I. After each bruising phone call, I'd nurse fresh wounds, alone with the baby in the cold apartment on Hoyt Street in Brooklyn. The infant slept through the screaming phone calls and bouts of shuddering sobbing afterwards. Or maybe I was mostly screaming and sobbing inside, not nearly as loudly as I thought I was. I could not believe that she would be so cruel to me. She must have sat in her own cavernous colonial two hundred miles north, Vermont's lingering winter crowding against the windows, and thought the same of me.

Except, of course, she was the mother. Maybe anything's permissible in maternal tactics if you think your child's life is at stake. And have no doubt, that's what she thought. She believed that I might not live from one day to the next in my urban setting. Her phone would ring, and a stranger's voice would inform her that my mangled body had been found. How could she sit idly by and allow this to happen? When I was a teenager she was fighting for my character and my reputation. Now she was fighting for my very life.

It kept getting worse. When the baby was six months old, I went back to work. She bought me a car. I didn't say this was simple. I commuted to work in that car and sometimes I drove north for the weekend, my son in a cradle on the back seat and later strapped in a car seat next to me. On some visits we didn't even fight. She was a wonderful grandmother: calm, patient, protective, and helpful. She never declined to baby-sit. She never gave much advice about how to diaper or how to feed. For someone who had raised four babies of her own, she was extraordinarily reticent at trying to guide my inexperienced hands. She just kept struggling for my soul. And I wouldn't give it, not an ounce, not an inch.

Four years went by: my son learned to walk, to talk, and to use the toilet. He went from a full time babysitter to day care to pre-school. Our visits to Vermont continued. The fighting abated along the way, and we would form our little family of three, sometimes augmented at holidays by the presence of one of my single brothers. Mom had built a new house a year after Dad died and given the largest bedroom to my nonagenarian grandmother. Mom regularly reviled her own mother for her maternal harshness, but Gram was a beneficent figure in my life. I would sit next to her for a half hour while she cooed over the baby and spoke vaguely of ancient memories before falling asleep again.

Then Mom and I would settle into the family room, and she would speak of her life as a widow. She talked about loneliness, the longing for male companionship, and her eventual repudiation of full time grieving, which she expressed, as was her manner, by switching from a Quaker affiliation to a Unitarian one. Once she spoke haltingly of her revulsion when a married man had come sparking about. Mostly, I was mute. I needed less to talk than to sink into the warmth of her living room and the competence of her well-utensiled kitchen on those weekend visits. The concept of her as a woman living a life parallel to my own seemed beyond grasping. She was more a mother figure than I ever cared to admit. So I listened silently to her tentative ramblings about her own existence, because I could think of no response. Perhaps my failure to interrupt was enough for her. I hope so.

16

Goodbye

Two weeks after my son's fourth birthday I attended a mixer at the Humanist Society on the upper west side of Manhattan and met Mark. From our first glances we were mostly together. It was mid-December. I announced to my mother that I wasn't coming north for Christmas. My reasons were foggy, but it had something to do with new love and with establishing the center of my life near my own home. My mother fell apart. We screamed and sobbed. She stopped speaking to me, told me so on the phone.

How could she? Again! I walked about my Park Slope apartment shaking with anger and shock. She was supposed to be happy for me. Three decades later I look back on my casual cruelty and wonder how I could have so easily not known that our holidays together were as important for her as for me. For God's sake, I was thirty years old already.

Mom put Gram in the local hospital and went off to northern Vermont to spend Christmas hanging around the ski resort where my younger brother worked. On Christmas Eve he phoned to report that Gram had died in hospital. At age ninety-nine she ended her snarled relationship with her own daughter in perfect timing to effect a reconciliation between daughter and granddaughter. And there was reconciliation. I invited my brand new boy friend to come with me to Vermont for the weekend, and he and my mother eyed each other cautiously, in preparation for their long, loving and respectful relationship. Okay, that particular weekend they remained vigilant strangers, but it was the beginning of an extraordinary connection that strengthened in time and contributed to the gradual extinguishment of the mother-daughter war.

So twenty-eight years later when I squeezed the clammy cell phone in my hand and called out to her, "Hold on! We're coming!" I knew that his presence by her bed would be almost as important as mine. The second call made us both mourners. The next day, after the cab ride, the airport, the flight, another airport, and a long drive up the Interstate through New Hampshire into Vermont, we arrived at her isolated, wintry house and joined more of the aggrieved: my brothers Duncan and Bill, my sister-in-law and nephew and niece, Chris and Erinn with their three small girls, and two of my cousins.

Crowds help, of course. So do funeral arrangements, wills, necessary notifications to relatives and friends, and condolence calls. Also mealtimes, traffic, TV schedules, and laundry. All that ritual and structure keeps reminding you that the world continues on in its impartial disregard, even when you rise at two AM and stand in the shower for an hour, because you can't think what else to do, to try to step outside time and just rest for awhile. Your little brother sits in a living room wing chair next to shelves full of elderly knick-knacks and stacks of books, his reddened eyes blank, and says, "If I could just sleep." Your son and his wife, both full time workers with demanding jobs, arrive and say, "Funeral in a week? Sure. We're here for the duration," and you start crying. Again.

He and his family disappeared from the house one afternoon, gone off for some time alone. At their return, we all sat around the bare dining table and listened to the children prattle. The two-and-a-half-year-old granddaughter turned a smiling face to me and urgently began a questioning chatter, pressing her inquiries in a babble of incomprehensible syllables. Finally my son broke in. "No, Ryan, this is Grandma Trish. It's Grandma Kate that died." The almost four-year-old, oldest granddaughter addressed her younger sister with exquisite condescension. "I *told* you, *she's* not dead." I laughed out of control, falling off my chair. Then the girls and I played again as we had the first night, hard tumbling and uncontrolled crashing about. My grandchildren must think that grief is manifested in hysterical behavior, that it is an occasion for silliness in adults. And perhaps it should be.

She lingered, I'm sure. Maybe she couldn't leave without communicating back to the daughter who'd finally spoken so freely over that phone in the ER. She always wanted the last word when we were fighting, after all. One slushy afternoon I went with my younger brother to the funeral home to attend to some necessary details. While he dealt with the wispy undertaker, I slipped into the drafty room where her coffin rested and approached that gleaming box to lay my hand at its head. An electric current shot through my arm and cemented my hand to the polished wood. I was grounded there, riveted beyond movement. Minutes passed. I didn't bother to struggle. She'd either let me go, or she wouldn't. She finally did. My hand was released back to my side, and I rejoined the two men in the lobby, where the funeral director jigged before me, speaking in gibberish. My brother waved the man away and led me outside to the car. We were silent for the ride back up the mountain. Night was coming on fast, turning the snow graphite under the leaden sky. Our loss, so long expected, so particularly right in the order of life, lay like a ton of black coal between us on the car seat.

I couldn't leave that house, the last of her many ones, the lair of her old age. M and I were staying at the local motel, but from early morning until bedtime I remained in her home, moving from room to room, seeking rest, talking to my brothers, hugging my grandchildren. M wanted me to return to the motel for afternoon naps. I refused. While the week lasted, we remained within her sphere. The jars of cumin, paprika, curry, and turmeric were still lined up in her kitchen. Opening the freezer to search for ice revealed a tumble of worn plastic bags holding wheat germ, whole-wheat flour, raw nuts and brewer's yeast. The whole house was dusty and cluttered.

It was unlike her to keep a dirty house. Six weeks earlier, during our last visit with her, I'd noticed the change. Dust coated surfaces. Spills weren't cleaned up. Dishes stayed soaking in the sink. My mother had been an exacting housekeeper, setting standards that I sullenly failed to meet from adolescence onward. My older brother, the one who lived with her, said he thought she'd given up after the death of her brother. Perhaps she had. Yet she'd seemed so happy with us in November. It's true that she didn't want to leave the house to go out to dinner, one of her perennial pleasures. But all the other signs were good: her bright eyes, her intense interest in discussing history with M, her gossipy conversations about neighbors and family. I still thought she'd reach the age she'd predicted for herself when I was little: "I'm going to live to be a hundred and two!"

There were slips. Twice she fouled up with the stove, leaving unused burners at searing temperatures. We bought her a microwave and set it up on her counter. She listened indulgently while M instructed her in its operation. Later M and I sat within earshot in the living room and heard her tell my brother with dignified condescension that this contraption was unnecessary and took up much too much counter space. The sound of their murmured collusion raised M's head from his book and sharpened my glance at him. We knew that she wanted to die at home, and that only my brother's presence every night allowed her to pursue this plan. "I just hope she doesn't die from a horrible burning," I whispered to my husband in a vinegary hiss.

For her whole life she'd taken great pride in her health, which she nurtured with a near obsession for healthy eating. Perhaps this was inevitable for a woman whose nascent college career had been cut short at age eighteen when polio confined her to bed for six months. That same polio marched back into her life as post-polio syndrome in her fifties, gradually crippling her. As she progressed slowly from one cane to two, to a wheel chair when traveling, and finally to a walker at home, her eyes and cheeks continued to glow, her hair grew soft and full, and her mind stayed sharp. Her heart had mellowed, and I'm not imagining this. All that sharp advice and demanding guidance of my early adulthood dwindled away. As we became increasingly protective of her physically, our emotional relationships teetered towards equilibrium. And it was "we", for M was a necessary part of the little triangle where we balanced. At first we three adults had oscillated around the two little boys, M's son and my son. Issues of loyalty and equality were hammered out. Love was proven on all sides. The boys grew into young men, and we discussed them as we watched them go. Nothing binds three parents more strongly than children. Nothing illuminates your understanding of your parent more than experiencing the same stages with your own child that they went through with you. My mother and I aged into greater understanding, grounded in my maturing children and her increasing infirmity.

And now she was gone. Too soon. If the person is more in the mind than the body, if the relationship lives in the exchange of ideas and perceptions, then much too soon. I wasn't done yet. Yet when my hand was released from that coffin, I had to walk on, learning different patterns with my brothers, finding a path with M through our mutual grief, becoming the matriarchal point in the constellation of my own children and grandchildren. We all had to give up that old lady's house on the side of a mountain in Vermont that had served as the family base for the last twelve years. We would no longer ask each other, are you going to Mom's for the holiday? The base was gone, and there was no sense of what would replace it.

The morning we'd arrived at the house on the mountain for the last, terrible week there, hugging and crying with my brothers, our dog had circled my ankles in a constant rubbing contact until I bent to acknowledge him. He leapt into my arms. I saw again what had been evident in November: he was poorly groomed and side splittingly overweight. Dogs had accompanied Mom throughout her adult life, a succession of them from the Springer Spaniels we'd kept when I was little up through the pair of Samoyeds who'd attended her widowhood. By the time the last Samoyed died, Mom had lost the agility to train another puppy. Murray was eight years old, not too big, alert but no longer a maniacal puppy, when she started her yearlong custody of him while we traveled. I told her she could keep him forever if she wanted. He was her chance to have her own dog again. Six weeks after taking him in, she decided to do just that. In November he'd been hysterically glad to see us, then had divided his sleeping time between our bedroom and hers. Now we had him back. I stroked his floppy ears and rubbed the curls on his back, just where my mother's hands had passed not days before. The dog formed a physical bridge back from death and into the solidity of life. Such was my idea, my comfort.

I didn't want to fly with Murray. I kept thinking about that caged boxer in the Miami airport, circling and crying in his imprisonment. M found a rental car that cost only a small fortune, and we smuggled Murray past the rental office and headed south. We stayed off of Interstates and wandered down the roads closer to the coast, through the shuttered beach communities of Delaware, along the Maryland and Virginia coastline buffered from the Atlantic by Assateague Island, across the Chesapeake Bay Bridge into the nautical clutter of Virginia Beach, and south to the top of Cape Hatteras. Here the season stopped us: there were warnings of ferry closings due to weather if we persisted down this broken continental edge. Mark turned the steering wheel due west on US 64 and headed for Rocky Mount and Interstate 95. He was doing all the driving, while I watched the scenery role by from the passenger seat. Skies fascinated me: high drifting wisps of vapor shifting colors as sunset approached, transparency at the horizons shading to thick blue on top of the dome, lumpy storm clouds forming far away to march threateningly forward. I had never felt so connected to the heavens.

We talked. I know we did. What we said was immaterial; the sound of his voice, easy and constant, drifts through the memory of those days. We talked, the miles went by, and the car cruised past the exit for Kingsland, Georgia, over St. Mary's River into Florida and down the long straight away to Homestead. When I opened the RV's door, Murray jumped ahead of me up the steps and bustled about from corner to corner, nose to the floor. How would we three manage in this small space? Could we comfortably add thirty-five canine pounds to the mix? We could and we did. Our caravan turned north and then west to head out along the flattened curve of the top of the Gulf of Mexico towards New Orleans. Thick memories of my parents crowded along the Mississippi coast, awaiting my arrival.

Thanksgiving, 1999: Erinn, Ryan, Mom, Katie and Chris

17

Boats On The Tide

The foggy hamlet of Bay St. Louis anchors the western end of Mississippi's Gulf Coast with a cluster of vacant looking buildings grouped alongside the shore drive and scattered haphazardly up the few roads that strike northward away from the water. The dreamy sense of desertion persists even after discovering that the buildings hold unpretentious restaurants, junque/antique stores, and even an art gallery shaped like a railroad car, with each compartment inhabited by a different artist. The town resembles many others on this obscure shore. The charm of its name had been singled out in a comment made by Mom during our last visit together. "Go to a little town called Bay St. Louis. I was really struck by it." She then handed me a copy of <u>Major Butler's Legacy</u>, by Malcolm Bell, Jr., with the remark, "This is one of my most important books." She closed her eyes and drifted off into a nap.

In late January the Gulf Coast drowsed through clammy days that began and ended in obscuring fog. Mosquitoes as big as dragonflies banged against our screens at Buccaneer State Park. Spanish moss swathed the toweringly bare trees. At night train whistles rose and fell in contemplative respirations from the tracks skirting the back of the campground. Murray and I walked daily out the park's half-mile access road to the edge of the Gulf and along the curving shore. All three of us piled into the car to drive slowly eastward back to Biloxi, watching the small, dirty surf at our right and the south coastal architecture on our left meander past. Murray napped on the back seat. M rambled on about southern history and gambling. I puzzled over my parents' lives, seeking clarity and answers in my neglected memories.

Their trip south was the first of their traveling decade, undertaken as my brothers and I left childhood behind. Mom and Dad would have been in their fifties then, late middle age, the time of surrendering children to their own independence and reassembling as a couple, of facing the need to reinvent the meaning of their lives. In that state of mind my mother had visited this coast, and one, tiny, fog-blurred town had stayed in her imagination for almost forty years. Maybe it was the artistic flavor: that string of galleries, those junk shops. Not so. The proprietor of the galleries proudly informed me that they were less than a decade old, established by artists gathering in the cheap shelter of the dying town's houses. So what could possibly have been here that stuck in my mother's memory for so long? She could romanticize the strangest things sometimes.

Innumerable unasked questions occur to one after a parent is gone. If only one had had the wit to ask them, full and clear answers might have been forthcoming. Mysteries would have dissolved, and now comprehension would be complete. Of course not. Our lives require some opacity with those closest to us. Children and their parents must keep secrets from one another. Generations carry on bloodlines, attributes, habits, prejudices and beliefs, making some changes, retaining some biases, and inflicting old patterns now grown irrelevant onto their progeny, all without calculated knowledge of what they do. It's designed to be that way, and perhaps it all depends on the maintenance of some obscurity.

I had spent my working life in mental health, a field that believes in the ability to transform oneself through gaining an intellectual understanding of one's emotional issues. Unearth and express the hidden contradictions, and one will approach freedom. At thirty I considered this to be received wisdom. By age fifty-seven the acid experience of the hurt that is so often inflicted in the process had corroded my allegiance to this principle. I set more store by tact and privacy than I would have thought possible when I graduated from social work school.

But whatever my maturing acceptance of the necessary mysteries between people might be, inside me the little girl stamped her foot and demanded to know about her own parents. What did they say to each other in the privacy of their car, motoring through Mississippi in 1959? My father had a decade left to live. He would not have known that, anymore than he could have foreseen us all go crashing through the sixties screaming our politics at each other. He couldn't anticipate the familial dramas of his own life that ran tandem to his nation's upheavals: his children's troubled exits from the home, his own collapsing health. When they were wandering about Mississippi and Alabama I was at boarding school, one of his sons had finished a stint in the Navy, and another son had just joined up. The southern trip was the first in a series that took them farther afield every year, through England and Spain and up the fjords of Scandinavia, until they had reached into Russia, eight years after they saw Bay St Louis. My own affairs during those years interested me too intensely to allow me to pay much attention to their recounting of their travels. Maidenly narcissism blocked the comprehension of most of what they told of their own lives. Some artifacts remained to illuminate my present quest to understand them, now that I had arrived at my late fifties. I have a black and white snapshot of them disembarking on an unidentified pier, accompanied by my aunt and uncle, their faces distracted and tense. The men wear coats and ties, the women step towards the lens in swinging skirts that hit mid-calf, high heels and pillbox hats, large handbags hooked on their arms. The foursome strides forward from camera left to right, making no eye contact with the photographer but aware of his presence. My mother's face is smooth with the relative youth of her fifties, and tense with the enmity she felt for her sister-in-law. My father's face already looks puffy and ill beneath his fedora.

And so I went on thinking, thinking, thinking of them throughout Mississippi and Louisiana. It was Carnival time, not yet spring, mild and grey and misty, soft underfoot. New Orleans seduced me right down to my toes: unexpected bottle rockets of jazz riffs bursting in the air of Woldenberg Park, to be answered by the shuddering responses of ships' foghorns drifting away down the Mississippi; the odiferous suggestions of gustatory climaxes floating out of alleyways; the air of complex bondage and constant decay that culminated in the softly looming cemeteries. Perhaps my mother's ability to romanticize had not been completely lost on me. In late afternoons the parades stuttered by, and we stood at the curb with the other tourists and derelicts to call out for bead strings and ersatz coins before heading back to the state park. Train whistles vaulted through my sleep, and one night I wakened and watched the whole procession of generations ride the sounding arcs, up into passing ascendancy and then gently down into the earth.

We left Buccaneer State Park and traveled north to Lafayette. I was deep into the book Mom had given me about Major Butler and his family's history as South Carolinian plantation owners and Philadelphia residents. On the one-month anniversary of her death we toured Shadows on the Teche in New Iberia, the home of four generations of a slave holding, sugar growing family. Forty-five white people and two hundred and fifty slaves lived on the food produced here. The verandah on the river side of the house faced a modest sloping lawn; but stately columns that ranged along the house's garden side created an air of grandeur. The peremptory woman guide told us not to be fooled: this was a working site where slaves slept on the ground floor, whites on the second floor, and the third floor provided storage space. From the look of the attic, this family never threw anything away. The original owner went to Boston during construction, seeking medical help for his "complaint." From there he shipped back piles of furnishings, before dying without having ever returned south. Some years later one of his sons, aged 38, was found wandering in the garden (picture long rows of cabbage, not rose bushes,) out of his senses. Brought to the house, he died two days later. During the Civil War the Union Army occupied the first floor, and the original mistress confined herself to the second floor, where she expired in 1863, to the sound of military boots and the smell of campfires and gunpowder. Her great-grandson had dedicated the last thirty-six years of his life to restoring the place. I wondered what he managed to discover about his family's mysteries and what was left unknown to him at his death.

The month of whispering Kaddish, Jewish prayer for mourners, was at an end. I put on makeup and jewelry, and we went to Prejean's in the town of Lafayette to feast on venison sausage, crawfish etouffe, dirty rice, corn with sweet seasoning, and Jack Daniels bread pudding. In twenty-four hours the temperature dropped from the muggy eighties to the raw forties. At nightfall we heard gunfire, followed by the deep barking of serious dogs. Murray begged to go out into the darkness. He raced around at the end of his leash, crying softly in his throat, then spun about and headed back for the lights of the camper, where he sat shivering on the couch and listening intently to the world outside.

For our last southern sightseeing before crossing into Texas, we took a swamp tour. The flat bottomed boat nosed through a landscape of silvered tree trunks, their tops reaching towards a lead sky, their feet planted in the emerald green duck weed that covered the water's surface. Hundreds of spectral birds flitted amid gray tree trunks, bleachy white shapes drifting on invisible currents and flicking back into the unseen distance. The guide bumped the boat up against a tangle of roots at the shoreline, dipped his hand into the maze of lumpy limbs and came up with a baby alligator, ten inches long, brightly marked with red and green slashes against black. Its mother, a nine-foot long knobby protuberance breaking the jade surface next to the boat's aluminum hull, raised her head to hiss and whistle a warning through an impressive display of teeth. Otherwise, she patiently awaited the return of her baby, while it was passed from human hand to hand. Finally the guide slipped the youngster back into the water, and Mom sank underneath the duckweed and surfaced a little farther away. "You better guard those babies," our Cajun guide remarked to her, as we drifted away. "Two days ago she had five, now I only see three," he explained. "Someone's eating them." The beast flipped her tail at us in a goodbye splash. Every mother makes her own decisions about what endangers her children and what doesn't. She isn't always right.

On February second we rolled onto the rough concrete of the Lone Star State highways, headed for San Antonio. Here our campground lay out beyond the rodeo grounds next to a wild brown river littered with trash at its shoreline bends.

A group of Germans in rented camping vans clustered at the rear and talked loudly to each other at their picnic tables. Otherwise the muddy landscape was deserted. The field across the street from the campground held lines of empty livestock trailers. One afternoon we visited the rodeo and wandered through the hangar size buildings, looking for the occupants of these trailers. Instead we found rows of display booths selling leather, jewelry, wooden kitchen implements, and Indian artifacts imported from Indonesia. In response to our questions concerning the animals, we either got a vague wave of the hand or the suggestion to return in the evening. Maybe we Easterners just couldn't 'get' the rodeo. I met a woman on the city bus headed for the fairgrounds who could hardly contain her excitement. She looked to be in her thirties and had a dark eyed prettiness that provoked a certain surprise when learning that she was off on her jaunt alone. But she was doing just that, a San Antonio resident spending her day off from work going to the rodeo and bubbling with the anticipation of it. I liked her a lot.

The city itself pleased me the most in the arches of the rough walls at Mission San Juan and in the flavors of a lunch of chicken and vegetables in broth at Mitera, followed by sweet potato in a thin sugar crust. A single day of transparent blue skies broke the iron chill of February, before the weather returned to wintry hues. The cold drove us back to the RV early each afternoon, where the warmth of our lamps distorted the sense of time. My reading picked up speed. I went through Barcester Towers, (Anthony Trollope,) The Man in the Queue, (Josephine Tey,) and Memories of the Old Plantation Home and a Creole Family Album, (Laura Locoul Gore.)

Maybe it was all the reading, or the cocoon of the RV, that provoked vivid dreams as entertaining as the movies. At night I returned to work with former colleagues, who involved themselves with me in fantastic plots. Responsibilities were heaped on me and then snatched away, situations developed that made me giggle in my sleep or caused my heart to race with anxiety. Just as suddenly, a dream would turn and I'd be walking Murray near my Brookline home, then chasing him as he ran away down a country road towards the southern Vermont house where I'd lived before going off to boarding school. I would enter and find myself in a strange kitchen with a huge bathtub in the middle of the floor. Waking, I'd recognize the laundry room and the black laundress who sat ironing in it as being from the first house I remember, in Portland, Maine, when I was two. I close my eyes again, and Murray is beneath the water near the pilings of an old wharf. M and I search frantically for his head. A man walks along the shore; it's my father, young and slim. And on and on the night visions tumbled, like a private tour, or a treasure hunt for just me. I went to bed earlier, slept later.

The RV had maintenance scheduled in San Antonio. When that was finished, we hooked the car to the back of our home and turned west with vague ideas of New Mexico. In less than four months we were scheduled to be at my mother's interment in Vermont.

M, age seven, with a friend

18

Bend in the Road

Mark was a child in the fifties, when even little Jewish boys living in Sunnyside, Queens owned a full cowboy outfit. A cracked black and white snapshot shows him at seven years old, standing with a less fortunate friend on a narrow balcony. A tipped back ten-gallon hat frames M's tough hombre scowl, while his right hand cradles the butt of a holstered revolver. His vest and flaring chaps are decorated with tassels and steers' heads. Fifty years older, rolling over the Texas border, his thoughts turned to the towns of Corpus Christi and Laredo. With no clear idea of their modern day incarnations, he was still pretty sure that the soul of cowboy Texas resided somewhere in them. I traced the mileage of the detour we'd have to make to reach them and tried to think of arguments that might dissuade him. After all, no one had given me a cowboy outfit when I was a girl. I hadn't felt that magic weight against childish hips. Surely the rest of the state of Texas held more easily reached places of cowboy evocations. "The thing is, my dear...," and just like that, he gave them up as destinations. We trundled on along Interstate 10, stopping for our first night west of San Antonio in the town of Junction. The wire thin man in the combination living room/office said, "I tell people, if you're looking for something to do, keep going." Two morose middle-aged women walked back and forth between the office and their camper with a broken down engine, hoping for news that a tow truck was on the way. Each time they returned to their elderly camper, their chins sank lower on their chests. We pulled out at seven the next morning.

The highway had entered the huge and subtle prettiness of Texas hill country. Road cuts revealed the striated layers of ancient ocean bottoms. Hundreds of delicate, steely windmills swung their needle arms about haphazardly in witness to the capricious air currents. Hoary cacti raised battered silhouettes at the top of rocky washes. The wind thundered constantly against all sides of the camper, rattling us into exhaustion. At 2:30 we gave up and stopped in Stockton, where a transplanted Australian in another living room/office oversaw a severe campground stretched across the top of a windy hill and dotted with dozens of tree shaped sculptures. Closer inspection revealed these figures to be real trees, all cut off clean about twenty feet from the ground, their pewter trunks ending in thick flat stubs that might support the coffee cup of a giant. The campground map indicated, in addition to the laundry and the dump station, a rock garden. It was just that, a pile of dusty rocks. Australians are rumored to have a weird sense of humor, aren't they?

We passed time studying the map. Due south of us a purple border circumscribed a large triangular block where the Rio Grande River turned from a southeast direction to a northeasterly course: Big Bend National Park. We'd missed Laredo and Corpus Christi, how about a detour to this unfamiliar National Park before we cantered out of Texas into Arizona?

Route 385 was a two lane, deserted macadam strip headed due south for ninety-eight miles through the inevitable wind, nothing in sight on the flattened earth except the occasional distant low ranch house. We kept going into the level space in front of us. Thirty-five miles north of the park the outlines of mountain peaks began cutting up against the horizon. The sky was hard blue above us but softened by the dancing light of distance and atmosphere where the mountains stood.

Big Bend. We fell silent as we peered forward at the mountains jutting higher and delineating out into layers of irregular profiles. We were still rolling along the ruler-straight road when the entrance hut came into view, and a park ranger in beige blouse and round brimmed hat appeared beside the driver's window. Yes, our National Park Pass, bought months ago at Race Point in Cape Cod, entitled us to free admission. Yes, there were campgrounds in the park, but at the moment they were full. Here was a map; if we drove through to Study Butte we might find private camping there. Enjoy the park.

We crept forward along the dipping, turning road towards the fantastic heights. Against a cerulean sky, color had washed out from this landscape to leave behind pure shapes of natural architecture carved in sharp and sinuous lines. The road entered the mountain range, and individual mountains began to stand away from each other, gaining girth, tilting the road surface in and out of the light as we rounded bends. In awe we made our way to the town of Terrelingua, as it was marked on the map. This was the place the locals called Study Butte, pronounced with two long Us. A private campground sprawled up the undulate foothills north of the road, kept company by the post office and a general store. We thought we had come for a couple of days; we stayed for ten.

Just before daybreak the profiles of the mountains to our east seemed cut from age-darkened tin, overlapping flat sheets differentiated by their random, jagged edges, floating just above the ground. Then the sun would twinkle at a high pass and rise above the metallic horizon, colorizing the sky to a throbbing blue and converting the weightless outlines into massive rock tonnage. Curvatures, canyons and mesas piled up against each other. Rounded foothills humped at the base of mountains that rose to peaks carved into crowns of vertical cliffs. A landscape first seen as colorless by eastern eyes began to yield its subtle palate after a few days: rust, gray, whites, beiges, muted black, purples, tans, soft yellow and sage blue greens; all scumbled together under the saturated sky. The eroded beige and gray edges of sandstone cliffs punctuated the high plains between the mountain. At night this whole variegated array sank back down into black, leaving behind a sky shimmering with the quantity and variety of its stars.

As a girl in rural New England I remembered such stellar displays, but not since. We bought a star book and a computer program to teach ourselves the constellations. I studied the pictures and then gazed bewildered at the twinkling carpet above. My first ability as a child to locate the Big Dipper thrilled me. In later years the Little Dipper also became a familiar in the sky, along with the evening star and Orion's Belt. Now all of those celestial markers disappeared into the mass of lights scattered across the black. Stars seen sparsely in skies softened by man-made light appear in gracious scarcity, allowing the comprehension of familiar patterns. This profusion above southern mountains denied any attempt to find those designs. Instead of seeing more of nature's order, I saw less. I sought more competence in my observations; I ended feeling overwhelmed and confused.

The daylight landscape was gradually gaining some small familiarity in our explorations. Across the Rio Grande's narrow, greenish waters sat Mexico. Near Santa Elena Canyon, we watched a rider on a muscular mule trot smartly down to the opposite bank to capture a maverick cow feeding on the lush grass by the river. When the three of them had disappeared up the dusty southern hill, I tossed a rock across the river, to hear it thud in the dirt and watch a small cloud of Mexican earth puff briefly in the crystalline air.

Santa Elena Canyon was slightly west of our campground, out along Farm to Market Road 170. After this stop, we continued out another sixty-seven miles along the route's dips and curves that tracked the river to the town of Presidio. On the deserted road the reflection of an old pickup looming suddenly in our rear view mirror felt vaguely threatening. At the top of a hill the truck swerved around us and disappeared down the pavement into the glittering air. For the next fifty miles the only other vehicle we saw was a white Border Patrol SUV, going fast in the other direction.

In Presidio we visited Fort Leaton, where wall displays of sketched maps and spare paragraphs in the small museum tell the cryptic story of Ben Leaton, a man of questionable business practices with a reputation as a scalper. In this tale of archaic criminality, apparent double crossings amongst his family and associates during the mid eighteen hundreds resulted in at least two murders. His son committed the second murder, probably in revenge for his father's killing. The young male guide sat nearby, alone in the deserted fort and blind in one eye, his thin neck bent over paperwork, letting us read the displays in silence. When he saw how we'd signed the guest register, however, he lit up. He'd recently taken his family on a trip to Boston. "I wanted my son to see the places he's studied about in school. And my brother lives on Cape Cod. We went whale watching there, from that town, what's it called, Provincetown? My son got seasick. The whales were something, though. I took my son to F.A.O. Schwartz there in Boston, it was almost time to close. I told him he could pick one thing. Anything. He said to me, "Dad, I'm overwhelmed." The ranger paused in his happy description, tenderness bringing a mist into his eyes. "Anyway, it's a great city. I want to go back someday."

"I love your area here also," I told him. I had my own naïve observations of his familiar environment. In answer to my questions, he explained the difference in cactus types that produced varying colorations, and the reason the river looked so small compared to its mighty reputation. We chatted happily, sharing our delight in discovery of each other's common reality. M and I wished him well and drove into town to lunch at the Mexican restaurant there. I finished the meal with a cup of flowery chamomile tea, the best I'd ever drunk. Maybe it was the air, or maybe the leaves in the small white pot were only distant cousins to the ones I bought in paper packets at the supermarket. Enchantment peeked around the corners of this whole area.

I drove on the way back to Terlingua, accelerating into the road dips so that our stomachs would flip as I swooped back up each rise. Halfway back we stopped at an empty movie set of small huts built on a steep slope on the river side of the road overlooking Mexico. The hut walls appeared to be real stone, but they were actually fiberglass panels fastened to particleboard. We opened one hut door to find a gleaming white toilet, a roll of toilet paper beside it. All the structures of the set stood unharmed. In other places, tumble down ruins of real stone huts dotted the hills, attesting to humans who had been here and moved on.

Near the campground a larger building with its roof still intact proved to be an old movie house, built shortly after talkies were invented and deserted before cinemascope came into vogue. It now served as a restaurant with a rather ambitious menu, where I ate venison sausage, jambalaya, and raspberry cobbler with bourbon cream sauce. The manic waitress delivered a synopsis of the area's history, telling us that the main draw had been mining for cinnabar, which is converted to mercury. The need for this substance fueled boom times for the area during World War One, eventually drawing a population of over two thousand souls and supporting the establishment of the movie house. The mine went bankrupt in 1942. The economics of destruction in World War Two did not crave cinnabar at the same rate. The waitress raced off to chat with another table.

Each day we went out to explore the enormous National Park. One drive took us to the Sotol Vista Overlook, where the deserted buildings of Homer Wilson's ranch were crumbling back into the earth in the canyon below. M and I walked separate ways out along the path that overlooks the remains of Homer's long ago efforts to sustain life in this treeless, rock-strewn place. No birds sang, no insects buzzed. My ears, so accustomed to their ceaseless task of filtering and sorting noise, could hardly stand the stillness and sought to create noise where there was none. Was that the hum of insects? Or just the blood behind my eardrums? The awareness of the lack of sound waves lapping against the eardrums was almost tactile, as if touch were standing in for hearing, reassuring me of the continued existence of all five senses. The fright that comes with sudden comprehension of one's irrelevance was quickly replaced by an engulfing calm, just disquieting enough to turn me back on the path. The sound of my feet clattering across the stones restored a measure of familiar proportion to the surroundings.

In the enormous visibilities of the mountains we fell into long peaceful silences between us. One day we crossed the park west to east, past Santa Elena Junction, Chisos Mountains Basin Junction, Panther Junction, Dugout Wells and Rio Grande Village. The ranger at the Maverick Junction park entrance had told us that there was a search and rescue operation underway for a hiker who had gone missing the day before. She wanted us to know that we would see helicopters, and Rio Grande Village was closed. So we passed the village and pulled into a dusty side lot just big enough for a dozen cars. From here the trail to Boquillas Canyon twisted up over a steep rocky hill and then dropped down through uneven landings into a grove of eight-foot high bamboo stalks that clacked in the wind coming from the canyon's mouth. Here the river curved into roiling currents and disappeared into rock face beyond the end of the trail. On both the US and Mexican sides the rock walls rose vertically, choking off any further progress by determined hikers. I stood gazing into the cleft, exhilarated by the rattling bamboo, the unreachable walls and the sense of isolation. Behind me M came around the trail's last bend and spoke with sharp disgust. "You shouldn't go on ahead like that in a place like this. You should have better judgment." He was probably right. We turned back together.

At the crest of the trail a scarecrow of a man walked towards us, his wiry form clad in clothes gone all to one shade of dust. "Hello," he called in a rising tone, as if greeting old friends he had unexpectedly stumbled upon. In a voice that suggested a difficulty with the hard consonants, he told us, "They found that hiker. He's okay, they got him in time. Took him out with the helicopter, he'll go to the hospital, but he's okay. Just some exposure." His excited tone implied a community effort and community relief at the outcome. The three of us balanced at the trail's peak as he chatted on, answering polite questions with clear disclosure and conveying his pleasure with the Park. He had moved to the area on April 17, 1995, and before that he had lived in Dallas for eighteen years, so he considered himself a native Texan. He worked for one of the vending companies in the Park, the same company he'd worked for in Port Angeles, Washington. A good company. They had transferred him here from the northwest. Today was his day off. He often hiked this trail on his day off. Balancing on a rock, he pointed down at the river far below us, to a log in the water. "See that? It's been here since last summer. Looks like a cow, don't it? One day it'll just be gone." Where were we from, he inquired. Boston. Abruptly, he turned away and waved goodbye, conversation over. We started back along the trail towards the parking lot. Fifty feet on, our temporary friend turned back to us and raised his right arm in a salute, or maybe a benediction. His voice carried on the wind. "I hope the Red Sox have a better year."

We drove back to the campground over the swooping park road. I began to sing out loud the old Bobby Darin tune that had been humming in my brain: "Somewhere, beyond the sea, waiting for me, hm, hm, oh yeah yeah,—and we'll go sa-a-ailing." M joined in, and we opened our throats full throttle to go on to "O beautiful for spacious skies,' and finally "O say can you see, by the dawn's early light." Big Bend had worked magic on the twisted kinks inside me, letting tension flow out in a soft exhalation into its enormous silence. Every pre-dawn dog walk started another day of immersion in the immense subtleties of dry color shadings, and the winking, glittering light. Barely awake, I'd step down onto the hardpan earth and wander along the edge of the foothill that backed the campground, turning to observe the growingly familiar shape of the boundary between mountain and sky and feel small puffs of warming air on my cheeks, while Murray explored the dust. One morning a thought flashed in my head like a sign blinking on: It's all coming together. What's coming together? The sign didn't specify.

Fort Leaton, Presidio, Texas

Murray

19

A Dog and Three Conversations About Home

We rumbled up through west Texas, two people and a dog sharing space and time. Big Bend's peace stayed with me, but Murray's contentment was rapidly dissolving in the growing heat of the Sonoran Desert in March. Back home he liked burrowing into snowdrifts. Here in the land of cacti, spines of all sizes awaited with vegetal glee for the arrival of his footpads. Lifting his leg became a hazardous occupation, injuring more than his dignity. Our walks grew shorter, by his choice. Finally, he refused to go outside altogether, until desperate to answer nature's call. His eyes patiently asked, what are we doing here? Our routine at home included a morning walk, a long daytime nap, an afternoon visit with our friends in the grassy park, dinner, and couple of drowsy hours before bedtime. It was perfect. Now the humans seemed to have lost their minds. Can't we just go home now?

The dog took a stand. He went under the table, lay down in the far corner and stayed there. And stayed there. He stopped eating. Once a day he allowed himself to be coaxed into a quick turn outside. Otherwise, he would wait beneath the table, thank you, until we came to our senses. By the time we got to Elephant Butte State Park in Truth or Consequences, New Mexico, his urine showed a tinge of pink. He was literally bleeding. We found a veterinarian in the yellow pages.

Back in Boston we take Murray to the local SPCA teaching hospital, a six story building on Huntington Avenue in Jamaica Plain. The parking lot is always full of Volvos and BMWs, and I can wait more than a month for an appointment. Once there, I stand in line at the first check-in desk while a young clerk with multiple rings in her ears and nose examines our account, and I examine the racks of pamphlets about grooming and car safety. Meanwhile Murray ecstatically greets the other patients. Financially cleared, we move on to the desk that feeds the examination rooms, where the staff members wear badges and talk brightly to the animals. Murray sets his heels here and has to be dragged into the exam room, where he affects a dramatic trembling from ears to tail. A resident from the veterinary school arrives, talking distracted baby talk to Murray while studying his chart. Murray never stops shivering until he can drag me out of there. If I report any change in canine habits, the doctor discusses possible esoteric diagnoses and the use of expensive diagnostic tests. Even without such testing, a bill of over a hundred dollars always awaits back out at the financial desk.

The vet's office in Truth or Consequences was a flat, one story building in a depression at the confluence of two greening foothills. Corrals on both sides of the long driveway held half a dozen sturdy horses that twisted their heads to watch our car pass by. Two middle-aged women wearing jeans sat at the reception counter inside. When I'd phoned, the vet himself had answered and given me a five PM appointment. He appeared in the empty waiting area: about fifty, solid wrists protruding from his white lab coat. "Mrs. Horowitz?"

"Yes." He gestured towards the exam room, and Murray trotted after him as though he lived there. Thick hands passed all over the small furry body, probing here and there, while my dog stood silently on the table, occasionally turning to look at the man's face. Human and dog gazed intently into each other's eyes. Then Murray gave me a dreamy look and lowered a meditative gaze to his toes, while the doctor poked his fingers deep into the dog's abdomen. In the end there was no definitive diagnosis, and we went away with a prescription to correct the ph level in his urine and a request to come back if he continued to pass blood. Murray left the small office and returned to his sunny outlook on life. He regained his enthusiasm for food, agreed to resume thrice-daily walks, and came out from under the table to demand regular petting sessions again. For forty dollars that vet restored the three of us to our happy days

The routines of the road flowed easily on. Yet still I wrote in my journal one day, I hope I have the strength to finish this year. I jerked from sleep one night, convinced that my snoring husband was a stranger. Breathe, breathe, just stay with your breath, you'll get through the night. Dreams swarmed in the dark, dreams I didn't want to have, recalling an ancient abortion, hoary fears of desertion, familiar faces twisted in unfamiliar rage. The peace of Big Bend had deserted me.

In Fort Davis, Texas, we had feasted at the bar of a crowded restaurant named Reata on deep fried jalapeno strips, crawfish quesadillas, steak au poivre, and pecan pie. A pinched young woman sat down next to us and chatted with the bargirl. They spoke of a sick husband. When the bartender had moved away, M asked, "Is you husband ill?"

"He got kicked in the gut three years ago by a steer. Messed up his intestines." Tears veiled her shy glance.

"He's in the hospital?"

"We just got back from the University of Nebraska Medical Center in Omaha. They have this nutritional program there. He had so many surgeries, so we tried this." She drew on her cigarette and brushed her bangs behind her ears.

"Did it work?"

"This team from Boston University came to work with him."

"Oh, BU is very good. They'll help him, I'm sure."

"I missed my family so much. We came home for a break."

"How long were you there?"

"He kept getting infections, he had to take so much medicine."

"How old is he?"

"Twenty four." Again tears puddled at her bottom eyelids. She lit a fresh cigarette and stared past the bar bottles. Laughter shrieked out behind us, and a man's voice bellowed across the room.

"So we came home for a break."

"What do the doctors say the prognosis is?"

Her eyes were red by now. "He's got a shot."

The bartender reappeared. "Hey, you oughta come shopping with us tomorrow."

"If I can get out." Her choked laugh drew the skin back over her cheekbones and exposed gritted teeth. Gray smoke puffed from her mouth, and we left her there to go back out into cool dark silence under the southwestern stars.

The next night at MacDonald's Observatory I spotted the Orion Nebulae through a telescope, but the Big Dipper still eluded me. At Gila two days later, we scrambled around the cliff dwellings, those ghost houses left behind by a people that inhabited the area in the late twelve hundreds before abandoning their dwellings and disappearing without explanation. These ancient human mysteries suggested a universal symphony whose illusive themes might cast my own movements into some perspective. But narcissism plays its own riveting tune. My parents and their lost secrets drummed in my thoughts. At night I lay in bed analyzing the pressure in my chest and trying to decide at what point I should rouse Mark and request that he rush me to the nearest hospital to treat a heart attack. At dawn I would wake to find my heart still pumping steadily away.

We spent four nights at City of Rocks State Park, south of Silver City, New Mexico. Here huge rocky monoliths lean vertically on each other and create twisting alleys that lead to hidden, deserted neighborhoods. Not unlike a geologic version of Boston's North End. Just outside this eerie village the Visitors' Center snuggles in a curving line against a dip in the land, its walls combining glass brick and beige adobe in a sinuous horizontal design that counterpoints the looming vertical rocks. The afternoon wind blew hard off the desert, flinging grit over everything, but in the mornings the air stood transparently still. Half a dozen campers were parked in the campground, standing distant and anonymous in the scourging draughts.

Cell phone service was fickle here. One afternoon I dialed my son, thinking to leave a message.

"Hello?" He sounded sleepy, or tired, or sad.

"Where are you?"

"In Brussels."

"Really!"

"On business."

"What's it like?"

"Oh, I only see the inside of the hotel, you know. But there's great smoked fish."

"How's the family?"

"I have to call the landlord. The unit next door is available. God damn, fucking-," and a stream of obscenities blistered across the satellite feed. "Erinn can't forget the fire, we need to be in the other unit, that family moved out. You'd think the fucking landlord could return my calls. They're showing the unit to strangers. I stuck with this guy, he could fucking have the courtesy to fucking return my calls." His voice rose, cracked. Then it flattened back into fatigue and sadness. "All I want is a home to come back to at night, just to go home after work and just be there, relax."

"I know, I know." This lame phrase was the best I could do for a response.

Earlier that day, we'd stopped for ice cream at a combination general store/post office in the town of Pinos Altos. While I ate a scoop of rum raisin I listened to two men talking by the stamp counter. "So while I'm on the Amazon, this tenant never pays his rent. He swore he did, put it in my mailbox, but I'd told him to pay Eddie direct while I was gone. He's always paid before, so I thought he was upright."

"Yeah, you'd think."

"Told me he couldn't afford to pay twice. Said the bank said his check had been cashed. So I say okay. But then Amy, down at the bank, says the check never came through."

"Don't know what to believe."

"I know what to believe. The guy lied. Guess I got to evict him."

We put down five dollars for our ice cream and left.

The next day we drove up and over the Black Range Scenic Area, to the town of Cuchillo's annual pecan festival. On a hill above town we ate our sandwiches leaning against the warm hood of the car.

"Massachusetts!" A voice rang out. Two men were climbing up the dirt road towards us, Laurel and Hardy mismatched sizes, both in their fifties, delight on their faces.

"That's right. Where're you from?"

"Hey, where you staying?"

"The state park, City of Rocks."

"Check out Deming. Coyote Park."

"Oh, we were in Deming before we came up here."

"Where'd you stay?" demanded the larger man.

"Near there, um, what was it? The Sunset?"

"Yeah, that's okay, but we got an indoor pool." The smaller man folded his arms over his chest and rocked backwards on his heels. "And a hot tub. You should come, it's great. Where're you from in Massachusetts?"

"Boston."

"Yeah, I got relatives there. Sunderland." The larger beamed at us, stringing out the three syllables. I glanced at M. We couldn't place it. The man shifted his feet and scowled slightly.

"North of Holyoke." He pronounced it Holly Hoke.

"Oh, sure, that's nice." Central Massachusetts is pretty, but then again I never heard anyone on the road ever say, "That place is ugly/boring/barren/etc." in response to a home place that another traveler had named. Everybody came from someplace of interest or admiration for fellow travelers, but there we were, all wandering around far from our homes.

"Yeah, yeah, they're having an easy winter. Forties, fifties. She's got relatives all through there."

The small man jumped determinedly back into the conversation. "We're from Pennsylvania. The southeast corner. It's warmer there than it is here right now."

"Yeah, when we left in December there was no ice on the lake, and my son says there's still no ice. My mother says to me, why do you have to go all the way out there? Doesn't make any sense." He laughed along with M and me. The smaller man twisted restlessly on his feet.

"We'd better go. The wives'll be waiting."

"But it's great out here, nice and clear," the larger man persisted. He talked on about cool desert nights and warm desert days. After a minute his companion walked off up the road in the loping gait of a small boy headed for home after curfew. The tall man reviewed the advantages of New Mexican weather some more. Then he flapped his hand in an abrupt farewell. "Well, check out Coyote Park. It's a great place. Our wives are gonna wonder what happened to us." He scuttled quickly off up the road to tell his wife about meeting people from green and beautiful Massachusetts, where so many of her relatives make their home.

Gila Cliff Dwellings, New Mexico

20

Homes Come and Go

Southern New Mexico's sere beauty, gilded with the beginnings of a desert spring, invited daily sightseeing. But I wanted to spend more time writing and drawing. The camper's confines restricted my efforts, as did my wavering self-discipline and M's sociability. He knew the morning drill by then and left me in silence with my notebook. Still the words came haltingly onto the page. I imagined that back home in my private study my creativity would flow forth. Then I worried that I was fooling myself. I reproved myself with the story of Jane Austen writing on a corner of the parlor table. If I were meant to write, piles of pages should be stacking up in the camper.

We traveled on to an enormous RV resort in Tucson. My younger brother forwarded a large box of our mail. Amid the bills, insurance notices, and credit card offers was an envelope containing the inventory list for Mom's house, assembled by my older brother as her executor so that we could each lay claim to what we wanted. Three single spaced pages listed items ranging from the beige corduroy living room couch to her ceramic lasagna pan. I could picture every worn possession. I poured over the list, marked it up, erased and marked again. I had to have this. And this. Wait. What if a brother wanted this? What if no one wanted this? How could we let it go? Once my mother had thought that all these things were so important. She guarded her Waterford crystal jealously and lectured us on the provenance of her silver serving dishes. Twenty years earlier, in her seventies, she had worried aloud about which child would inherit the plates hand-painted with lilac blooms, or the mahogany grandfather clock. In her last years, she dismissed all objects as unimportant. A question about a set of ancient dishes would elicit a shrug, and she would turn the conversation to politics, or family matters. But my brother's typed list named some articles that were iconic to me: the table that my father made for her, topped with dark blue, iridescent tiles they had bought together in Spain. A fat blue and white pitcher that had epitomized beauty to me when I was about five. A tall necked pewter vase with a curving handle that had sat on her dining room window ledge during all our chats in the last ten years. A print of an English swan pond, faded to obscurity, which had hung in every one of my parents' living rooms that I could remember.

Outside the RV's windshield residents of the resort strolled by in shorts. Inside, I perused my list, fell asleep thinking about it, and finally awoke one morning determined to finish my work with it. I mailed annotated copies to my three brothers along with a long note explaining my choices and stating that I would quickly relinquish anything, to avoid hard feelings. Please let me know, we should talk soon. Then I awaited their responses. None came. The phone and our email were silent. This apportioning of domestic objects just didn't matter that much to my brothers. I could have anything that I wanted. This had to be a gender difference. Their mother did not reside in the objects that she left behind. Home is something different for men.

Home never seems more powerful for M and I than in the early evening, when I've gone into the kitchen to start cooking, and he seats himself nearby to watch TV news and talk together. I pour us drinks, chop ingredients, and set up the morning coffee pot, sometimes dawdling in order to fill our ritual forty minutes. This daily interlude cements the surrounding ties that bind us. We've observed it wherever we've found ourselves in the last twenty years.

Yet in the camper I began to get edgy as evenings approached. Memories flicked through my mind of sitting in his parents' shag carpeted Florida condo, Betty laying out dinner dishes while Harry watched the evening news. Would M expect us to replicate his parents' marriage, as we got older? In the two decades that I had known his mother and father, through their seventies and eighties, they had been inseparable. My mother-in-law, New York City native, had never learned to drive. They filled their years in Florida with days punctuated by regular auto excursions to view the ocean, to eat out, and to shop, Harry at the wheel and Betty next to him. In between these outings Betty spent her days keeping house and waiting to see what Harry wanted to do next. At least that's how I saw it. I might love the hour with M from six to seven every evening, but I was terrified that he expected it to evolve into his parents' daylong pattern. I envisioned more freedom for myself. I had been waiting for more freedom and solitude all through the long working years.

Phone lines ran to each campsite at this RV park, and for the first time on the trip M enjoyed unlimited Internet access. He spent happy hours scanning the New York Times, the Jerusalem Post, AP wire, London Times, Washington Post, etc. We signed up to stay a third week. I swam laps in the three pools, attended yoga classes and drawing classes, and got my hair cut in the beauty parlor. Late afternoons I took Murray for long walks down the concrete drives. Happy retired folk pedaled past us on bicycles, hung on the edges of the hot tubs chatting, and gathered on cement pads in the early evenings to share brightly colored cocktails. They crowded the activities office in the services compound, waiting to ask questions about the lists of offerings posted on its bulletin boards. The order, stability and cleanliness of the place comforted us.

But something about the detailed schedules of available classes began to oppress me. Watercolor. Stained glass. Drawing for all levels. Write your memoirs. Woodcarving. Everyone aspired to be an artist in their leisure years. It offended my egoism. This was my special dream; it wasn't supposed to be the hackneyed goal of every retiree. The class lists reduced my creative longings to the trite and trivial.

We kept up our sightseeing: the Sonoran Desert Museum, Mt Lemmon, Sabino Canyon, and Old Tucson Movie Studios. I vacillated through the days, immersed in the vast southwestern beauty, claustrophobic in the camper and fitfully giddy with our freedom, aglow with the feeling of health that all the exercising brought on and panicky at night that I was having a heart attack, doing colored pencil portraits from photographs in People Magazine and anxiously anticipating my inability to develop any artistic pursuits. Grief still skewered me at odd moments, but hours passed when I didn't think of my parents. M and I laughed a lot at silly jokes and spoke more of what it was going to be like to go home. "Maybe as exciting as leaving," he suggested. That seemed improbable, but I loved his anticipation.

21

Who's Afraid of Death?

We had a fight. A savage blowout. It was about moving to Florida. He wants to. I don't. We were driving to the Biosphere, in Oracle, Arizona, with me at the wheel. I don't remember how the conversation started, but suddenly he was saying, steel in his voice, "No one's going to stop me from moving to the warm weather. I am not going to go on living through New England winters, even if that's what your family does." And I started screaming, right there on the highway with cars whizzing by in the sunlight's glare and my sweaty hands slipping on the wheel. We left the highway and drove down the long dirt driveway to the Biosphere. I'd stopped yelling, but my stomach heaved and my ribs squeezed my chest. I pulled the car in and turned off the engine.

"I don't want to be with you right now." My voice thickened in my throat. He promptly got out of the car and walked away into the heat.

Retirement makes you confront your own mortality. Don't deny it. Work all your life, get good at what you do, receive regular paychecks, and start all self-descriptions with your job title: I'm a social worker. A teacher. I sell. I write software. I run a real estate office. I make cars. I trade stocks.

Then stop. You can say, I'm a retired stockbroker, school principal, shoe manufacturer. So what? If you've stopped doing it, you've finished that part of life. You are that old. This is the last segment. I was that, now I'm not. That makes me a has-been.

People avoid retiring to avoid looking death in the eye. Those geezers who chortle away at the joy of continuing to labor as janitors, watchmen, or the like, you know, the ones that get quoted when the newspaper's Sunday style section or Modern Maturity runs an article on the new retirement, those bent, cheerful seventy-six year olds twinkling at the camera, let me tell you, they're all petrified of stopping the daily grind. They are the last-man-standing crew of the working world, the determined competitors who will never leave the field as long as one of them is still tottering in to the job. During my career I'd worked with a few of them. They made us youngsters crazy with their upbeat attitude about punctuality and their deliberately slow approach to every task.

The flip side of these aging combatants in the work world are the sophomoric gray-headed masses who populate Florida's fifty-five plus housing developments and long term RV parks, calling out hearty greetings as they rush off to golf and volley ball, wearing their leisure on their sleeves like newly besotted teenagers. That scene terrifies me, and that terror fueled my rage at M that day on Interstate 8. I might be frightfully ambivalent about returning to social work, but try even suggesting that I was closer in proximity to those aging hordes in the southern sunshine than I was to the ashen skinned laborers shuffling to work through the early hours of a northeastern morning, and I was instantly murderous.

A few minutes after M had left the car I walked up to the admissions booth and forked over seven dollars for one Biosphere ticket. No sign of my mate. Low structures in rounded off shapes lay scattered over a shallow valley and the hillside beyond. Looking and not looking for M, I wandered towards the largest one, on the crown of the hill. Other tourists rambled the pathways, moving about in pairs and groups. Alone, I climbed up to the Biosphere Observatory to gaze sightlessly at its exhibits under glass, then walked back down the hill to stop at the inevitable gift shop, glance in at the theatre, and consider the outside of the test module. Everything looked makeshift and slightly silly. Perhaps it was my mood.

It was lunchtime, and rage didn't cancel hunger. At the Canada del Oro, the Biosphere's fanciest restaurant, I ordered tomato basil soup along with a goat cheese and eggplant sandwich. When I was still employed I used to play hooky occasionally and walk into Boston for a luxurious day of shopping, a sensuously solitary lunch, and an arty movie matinee. Today's lunch turned to grit in my mouth. The trouble with being alone after a fight with your spouse is that you are not in the mood to enjoy the solitude.

I had stopped considering divorce. But the suspicion lingered that he was trying to trap me into something that I couldn't even talk about, much less plan for: retirement. True, this year off was supposed to be a testing of those waters. True, we sometimes spoke playfully of that distant time when work would be unnecessary. But that morning in Arizona, the make believe nature of our discussions had shattered before the wintry reality of actual retirement. Suddenly we were both fighting for our lives, convinced that the last remnant of our earthly years was about to be subverted and destroyed by our partner.

Because I wasn't yet ready for retirement. Sure, in my forties and for much of my fifties I'd been riven with envy every time I attended a retirement party. For days afterwards my spirits sagged. Summers were particularly bad. Dragging on work clothes in the early morning heat, I would see my life passing in a procession of wasted days. If I'd only had more imagination and courage, I would have been living some vastly more adventurous and productive life. In despair, I'd pull on a pair of pantyhose and shoulder my briefcase. The day's labor would fatigue me beyond despondency, until another dawn brought back the desperation in a knee-weakening flood. So why wasn't I clambering for retirement now?

The summer before, making our plans for this year of playing truant, we'd giddily contemplated our freedom. But since hitting the road my thoughts had persistently returned to work. A lot of my dreaming time was spent at the job: attending meetings, fighting adversaries, and making plans of action. Sometimes this nocturnal labor was frustrating, but sometimes it comforted and even entertained. In daylight my ex-colleagues peopled my thoughts during the long driving hours. Part of who I was required their presence, at least in my mind.

I knew that M was closer to accepting retirement than I was. He thought so also. A year or so earlier he had begun to talk to me about my workaholism. He saw this as an outgrowth of my family history. My father had inherited an income and never needed to earn a salary. His grandfather had built a decent fortune in the booming days of late nineteenth century Chicago and left it all to his two daughters. At his death they sold their shares to daddy's business partner and settled into the respectable lives of the fairly rich, the first and only generation to achieve this. My father's father never lifted a finger to increase the family's wealth. By the time my father and his brother grew to manhood, the inheritance supported decent middle class lifestyles for their two families.

But Dad was not a carefree man. He seemed to lack his own father's skill for the leisured life. Unexplained tensions and secret angry demons bedeviled Dad throughout my childhood. Everywhere we had lived he had established a workshop, a building separate from the house, where he spent most of his days. We children never entered this sanctuary of woodworking equipment. What brought him to this avocation, I have no idea. His own parents had shuttled languidly between a house in Pasadena, California and a gentleman's farm in Westport, New York. Old home movies show them wandering through their flower gardens at the farm, my grandfather in stiff high collar and dark tie, my grandmother in long dress and high button shoes. Spaniels chase about their heels while they bend proprietarily over peonies and roses. Later in the film the farm laborers can be seen doing the real work of the farm.

Without a tether to a job, my father was free to move his growing brood back and forth between coasts, until finally settling the family in southern Vermont for the last fifteen years of his life. Unlike his parents, he had a need to create with his hands, not just to wander gently through his gardens observing the fruits of others' labors. He built: stone retaining walls, lily ponds with small waterfalls feeding them, an acre of pristine ground cover, a rock garden, a tractor-tended vegetable garden, walls of stereo cabinets, coffee tables, gracefully turned lamps.

Dad is the lynch pin of M's theory that I've inherited a compulsion to work. M points out further evidence in my brothers, who fill their weeks from Sunday to Sunday with constant labor. Until recent years they never seemed to consider vacationing to be an accepted human activity. Are we all, as a family, somehow trying to redeem ourselves from the cloud of inherited means?

Working for a living has been necessary for me since my mid-twenties. M may be right that the Nash family's last two generations carries the burden to prove that they do live meaningfully productive lives. If such an unconscious force does run through our inheritance, I landed myself in a salaried life on purpose. I had started adult life with the unarticulated expectation, not unusual for the time, that I would wed and be supported by my husband. I married for the first time during the fifties end of the nineteen sixties, when life for women still meant pillbox hats, hair curlers, and girdles. Husband number one walked out in nineteen seventy, right in the middle of the messy decade that started with Dallas and moved on to the Gulf of Tonkin, protests, hippie summers of love, more assassinations, The Second Sex, and the incinerating explosion of anger between generations and classes. Alone with a four month old baby, I picked up the strands of my lackluster career in social work and began paying my own bills. And never looked back. Throughout the following love affairs, new friendships, a divorce agreement with child support but no alimony, and finally a second marriage, I took responsibility for providing financially for my son and myself. That meant steady work.

My mother called me a career gal, enunciating the diminutive last word through a gay, forced smile, her mouth conveying pride while her eyes telegraphed uneasiness. I would squirm and grow irritable under the description. I was a worker, dammit! A laborer, a wage earner, a provider. Her term for me indicated a choice, a life styling, an element of the optional. I worked because I had to. I provided for my son and myself. She should honor this without ambivalence. Except I don't think that she could. She saw our family as members of the moneyed middle class, whose women were measured by their ability to attract a man who would provide well for them.

In my callow self-consciousness I could not see the compelling plot line of her own life: a father who failed at most everything and died young, leaving her to live with and help support her mother until her own marriage to a man of means, then her years of competent industry as a housewife and mother. My young self was so proud of my salaried life. That pride grew more from my father's silent hours in his workshop than it did from my mother's daily labors for the family's needs. Behind all Dad's rantings at the labor unions and his lamenting of the difficulties of living on a fixed income, a shame seemed to lurk. Out in the working world I was attempting to expiate that shame, to prove that the family still carried the genetic forces that drove my penniless great-grandfather to leave Scotland behind and build a fortune in Chicago's food industry. I would prove that our family grit had not been sidelined by those gardens in upper New York State. So in some way my husband was right. If I stopped being a worker, I would let my father down.

Besides which, I missed the job. I emailed old colleagues, and occasionally they emailed me back. I thought intensely about newcomers on staff who arrived with their own ideas shortly before my exit. I knew the reasons those ideas wouldn't work and the dynamics and pitfalls they would only discover after being there awhile. I could have told them so much, if they'd only listened to me.

If I could have heard myself, I would have been amazed at how much I sounded like someone forced out, when in fact I had left triumphantly willingly, walking away from a group of jealous colleagues towards an enviable future. So what was this sense of being the kid outside the playroom with her nose pressed up against the window, painfully watching the popular kids' play? Had I really been of any value, if someone else steps in and does it without my help? Maybe, with me out of the way, it's being done even better.

Leaning over my tomato soup at the Biosphere, I thought less about my need to work and more about M and his determination to quit our ordered, employed lives and chuck the Northeast in the process. Loneliness tempered anger by the time I munched my way through the tasteless eggplant and cheese sandwich. I paid up and headed back to the car. In a few minutes he got in beside me.

"Hi."

"Still mad?"

"Yes. No."

"Me, too."

"We'll work this out." Our standard phrase for let's just let it go for a while. The fight had touched a third rail in our relationship. When it's just the two of you in a tiny camper, no other practical place to go, the best option can be to sweep something under the rug. We lifted the edge of the carpet and gave the whole mess a good shot with the broom. For now.

22

Time Colors Things

Tides of viridian and burnt sienna, ultramarine and cerulean, hooker's green and crimson, lemon and cadmium yellows flooded my dreams, tossing me on their prismatic surfaces. Fretful plots entangled themselves with the colors: friends betrayed me, and my efforts failed. If I could just drop below this restless surface into the oblivion beneath, peace awaited. I'd spent the previous evening with tubes of these colors spread before me on the table, muddling together combinations and painting the results down paper strips in the tonal graduations of an earthy rainbow. Our teacher called this exercise Watercolor Boot Camp.

I pushed up into wakefulness. Tuesday morning. The camper stood solitary behind The Inn in Abiquiu, New Mexico. Across the empty campground bright blue doors and window frames studded the russet walls of a collection of low adobe buildings, their foundations lined with an exuberant spring garden of forsythia, daffodils, grape hyacinth, iris, and creeping phlox. Pink and white flowering fruit trees bordered the driveway. Towering cottonwood skeletons walled off the back of the Inn's grounds from the straw-colored surrounding landscape. Beyond the trees, inky black cattle and their spring calves moved across the biscuit fields, bounded at their perimeters by sharp buttes shaded in purple, indigo, and rusty mahogany against the cloudless sky. At night all this beauty would fade to a blackness punctuated by the strings of tiny white lights in the Inn's café windows.

The previous week we'd traipsed around Santa Fe with three enthusiastic women from Indianapolis, following a slim octogenarian guide dressed in black from his tooled boots to his circular brimmed hat, who interspersed an impressionistic accounting of New Mexican history with personal stories of his children (11,) grandchildren (23,) and great grandchildren (8.) He had already outlived two children, one a daughter who'd been murdered by a shot between the eyes. He delivered this detail with the same crafty smile with which he told of the mysterious carpenter who built an unsupported circular staircase for the nuns at San

Miguel Mission Church and then disappeared without being paid. When the guide pointed out the Georgia O'Keefe Museum, my Hoosier friends could not contain themselves.

"You have to go to Ghost Ranch!"

"It's wonderful, wonderful! You can imagine her there. The country looks exactly like her paintings."

"And you can sleep there, too!"

As it turned out, we couldn't sleep there, because the ranch didn't allow dogs. We had taken my fleeting friends' advice and driven north the next day on US 84 to discover the jagged geology around the gleaming Chama River. The first green of spring hazed the riverbank trees. Every turn revealed a landscape that did look more and more like O'Keefe's paintings, until it seemed that nature was trying to recreate in open air the landscape that the painter had placed on gallery walls for the world to view. We drove in silence at twenty-five miles an hour, occasionally exhaling a Wow! Or a Whew!

Past the small sign for Ghost Ranch Conference Center we rattled up a roughly graded dirt road over a rise that gave on a view of low slung buildings scattered about the base of another display of sharp red cliffs pushing up against the ultramarine sky. A sign in front of the deserted main building informed us that the current owner of this old cattle-rustling station was the Presbyterian Church. Fliers in the somnolent little library advertised weeklong art courses in various media: catnip for me, but not the sort of thing that M had ever taken to. He took one glance and immediately chose a course in Deep Carved Pueblo Pottery, to be given the following week. Without hesitation I chose watercolor. We drove giddily back to Santa Fe to pack up the camper and bring it north to the Abiquiu Inn.

For the next five days we were apart more than we'd been in months. I liked missing M a little, looking forward to seeing him in the evening. Each morning was a rush of preparation to get us headed by eight-thirty up the road fourteen miles to the Ranch, where we joined the couple of hundred people gathered for a week of instruction and beauty. They had come from all over the country to eat the non-profit-budget fare of beans, salad and bread at communal dining tables. Ages ranged from the twenties to the sixties; jeans were the dress of the day. This crowd could have been the preachers' kids and teachers' kids from my boarding school days, all grown up. I met people from Santa Cruz, Maryland, Omaha, Denver, Minneapolis, Sonoma, Westchester, and New Hampshire. And a few who described themselves as locals, but these were all transplants to the area from elsewhere. They had wandered west, searching for something, and chosen this area for a new life. They spoke like giddy new proselytes of the expansive beauty and space.

My own thoughts narrowed down to water and color. After each morning's demonstration I sat in the back of the studio moving puddles of yellow ochre or cerulean around the paper, pushing impatiently with the brush or watching in alarm as the undulating stain suddenly flooded across the page. Our teacher, Pomona, circulated through the room in her uniquely cut denim tunics, a fluff of snow curls over her kind eyes, observing our efforts and offering unfailing encouragement. After a lecture on color that only muddied what I thought I knew, she assigned the mixing exercise that I spent Monday evening completing. On Tuesday we did value studies. On Wednesday she had us paint the surrounding cliffs, Georgia's scenery. Pomona supplied unflagging approval for my awkward blobs of sienna and crimson, but then told me that she herself had studied those same cliffs for two years before painting them for the first time. How could I ever...?

On Thursday Pomona loaded her twelve students into the ranch's aging van and took us on a field trip to the village of Las Ojos, a mountain hamlet about an hour north. A wool producing company dominates the tiny town. The sheep that provide the raw material live in pens behind a rustic showroom where a wall of cubbyholes displays knobby skeins that melt through fantastic ranges of hue and value. The class gathered behind the showroom to watch Pomona demonstrate the making of a field sketch. The reliable New Mexican sun created shadow patterns on the dilapidated shed that served as her subject. The wind tickled my hair about my nose. Two dogs, one tan mutt and one dark rottweiler mix, moved eagerly among the group, shoving their muzzles up against pockets and into bags. Canine memory informed them that this group must have lunch somewhere, just like the last group this white haired human had brought. With aggressive charm they claimed their share of the collective food.

Then we were let loose for two hours, to attempt our own field sketches. The whole village felt like a big house with outdoor hallways, the inhabitants walking by and saying where's Pomona? Oh, she's in the store now. No, she went out back of the woolen shop a minute ago. I think I saw her stop by the gallery over there. The exuberant dogs continued to ricochet about. Suddenly something caught their eye across the north field, and they catapulted simultaneously over an old fence in one choreographed leap and disappeared into the brush. Nearby one of the local men had been chatting with Pomona about his genealogical search on the Internet.

"This must be heaven for dogs here," I remarked.

"Not really. Most of these dogs don't belong to anyone, like those two; people put them out when they get full grown, to fend for themselves. The sheep ranchers shoot them all the time, and sometimes they don't make a clean shot, and the dog bleeds to death. Or they get hit by a car and end up crippled, or lose a leg in a trap. I've been feeding that big one, but then of course he attached himself to me, and my own dog gets offended." Whatever the grim fate that awaited them, the bobbing heads of the rowdy strays in the tall grass spoke of their present gaiety. Mindless of the future, they could live each day fully before death or dismemberment caught up with them.

Pots At Ghost Ranch Waiting To Be Fired

By Thursday evening I was exhausted, and we were beginning to speak of where we would go from here. Mark's group made plans to go out to dinner and then take a nighttime tour of some nearby Indian sites with their Pueblo teacher. They had spent half of their week touring the area, while waiting for their pots to move through the various stages of firing. This involved cow dung, which gave the pottery its distinctive blackened coloration. On Tuesday, after a full day of shaping clay, M had sat at dinner and laughed, a little embarrassed. "I can't stop thinking about my pot." On Wednesday, after a trip to Bandolier National Monument, he had said, "I'm talking about Kabala with them, Kabala and Indian mythology." He only discussed religion when he felt strongly connected to people. Over dinner we chattered about our fellow students and our class curriculum. His sudden bonding with his teacher and classmates paralleled my own immersion in color for the week. Silly excitement hummed through our evening conversations. But tonight I would be alone, while he ate Mexican food with his new friends. Perhaps I'd be lonely.

It was wonderful. Solitude settled like a warm blanket on the dog and me. I moved freely back and forth from one end to the other of our traveling house. The only sound besides the slight clatter of dishes and art materials was that of a car passing every few minutes on the road three hundred yards away. After a long saunter around the grounds of the Inn, Murray fell asleep on the bed. I showered, cooked up a bowl of fusilli with peas, carrots and sharp cheese, and got into bed to read and spoon warm pasta into my mouth, the dog pressed up against my thigh. My eyelids drooped, then widened again; my focus drifted on and off the page. The sound of cars passing on the road had ceased. Nothing else broke the stillness. I laid down the book, but left the light on. Around ten o'clock a far off murmur resolved into the sound of an approaching engine. A car door chunked open, voices spoke indistinctly. M was home. I fell from my drowsy vigil down into dreamless sleep.

Friday afternoon we still talked happily of our Ghost Ranch week, but now the future needed puzzling out. We laid out the route to Monument Valley. Saturday morning I awoke at six and walked alone across the paved highway to climb the rutted dirt road that cut obliquely up the hill towards the village of Abiquiu. I wanted to see if I could make it all the way to the home where O'Keefe had spent her summers. Near the top of the hill a man drove through the gate of his chain link fenced yard and got out of his car to refasten the padlock. He stared at me a little hard, and then we nodded in the country way. Behind the fence a chesty German Shepard barked at me, showing his large incisors. I walked on into the town square, dominated by an adobe church with a plain white cross atop the steeple. Early morning sun sliced through the square to illuminate the church's eastern wall. On the far side of the square a man came out of a doorway and placed a chair against the glowing clay. He sat down and gazed steadily in my direction. To my right a low adobe wall protected the yard of Georgia O'Keefe's village home. The electric switching box that one of my classmates had told me about stood midway down the stretch of this barrier. With the morning birds and the silent man as witness, I climbed up and peeked into the yard. Spring's green richness highlighted the soft russet of the house. During O'Keefe's life vegetables must have sprouted where now there was lawn. Content with my small, secret discovery, I descended from the box and started back along the dirt road.

Behind the house with the fence a dog barked steadily. The man must have tied him up. That was a serious dog, and I was kind of glad. Drawing alongside the fence, I saw that I was wrong. There were two dogs, the one barking and the one that I'd seen before. This dog did not bark. He raced back and forth by the fence, launching his body against the metal netting and making guttural sounds in his throat. The links squealed under his assault. His murderous frenzy compelled my gaze, watching for signs of the fence's collapse, but I forced my head away to avoid challenging him further. Rocks strewn in the road tripped my faltering feet, and my knees threatened to collapse. Clumsy and rushing, trying not to break into a run, I fled down the hill. "I hope that fence holds you," I muttered to myself. Stones rattled away from me, and the dog's body thudded gratingly against the metal links. I thought, he knows where the hole is that he can get through. He knows and I don't. Any second now he'll be in the road with me. Finally we reached the far angle of the yard. He hurled himself against the corner post and at last began to bark. I continued my flight down the hill for another two hundred feet, escaping his snarls. My underarms prickled and the back of my neck had yanked to rigidity. I believed that Shepard's farewell message. If he could have gotten through the fence he would have killed me. Do not walk this way again. Okay, I won't.

During our stay in Abiquiu the daffodils and tulips had faded, but the purple iris were coming on strong. The green haze on the trees was resolving into defined leaves. A tender red glow had begun misting the bushes around the cow pasture. We were still the only camper sitting behind the Inn, but there were more signs of life on the property. Cars parked next to the cabins and stayed overnight. Occasional strollers passed by our site. On Saturday afternoon two men and a woman stopped to chat, accompanied by a ragged wolfhound mix that took an instant liking to Murray. These people were transplants, living here for years, but not natives. The woman's bony wrists and ankles stuck out of her floppy clothes. She'd come from Topeka and lived here for ten years. She squinted as she told of separating from her partner, giving up her interest in their shared house and deciding to return to Kansas. "You know, the locals don't want us living here. They still burn people out around here." Or keep dogs that convey their own messages to strangers, I thought to myself. I hadn't told M about my morning encounter. His protectiveness might encroach on my freedom.

Our twenty-fifth wedding anniversary had passed in Abiquiu. M and I often forget the date until it's upon us. I'm not lying; I do too. M's father taught him a deep suspicion of all holiday celebrations. There's no explanation for my heedlessness. The first few times it happened, it made me nervous. Perhaps it signified some lack of gravity in the marriage. Later I chose to take it as a sign that we didn't need a yearly acknowledgment of our bond. Judaism holds that the holiest day is the weekly Sabbath, not the annual festivals. Our life together counted its meaning in the march of days, not the marking of years.

The fight at the Biosphere remained unresolved. Somewhere back in the muddle of the last decade our marriage had reached that point where the partners gain the confidence that things will work out in a way that each can live with. Lucky marriages get there after a certain number of crises that teeter the spouses at the brink of divorce. We'd done that.

So it might help to know that we had that commitment as we faced the puzzles of the future, but that didn't supply any answers to those dilemmas. The week offered clues to what I needed from our structure in the future: the mutual desire to learn, the lack of loneliness on Thursday evening coupled with an anticipation of his return, the instinct to keep silent about the dangerous dog in order to preserve my walking freedom. But clues don't create a reality.

I married him because he made me laugh. That is my one constant reply to the question, why? Other answers have come and gone, not that one. Laughter got us through a lot. We hadn't yet seen the funny in our differing expectations of the future.

Abiquiu Inn, Abiquiu, New Mexico

23

Monuments to Memory

I stood smiling and writing in the darkness of the Visitors' Center at Monument Valley Navajo Park. Here's what I copied onto the backs of postcards:

First World-Black World

The first world was inhabited by the Holy People/Insect People. Man was not in his present shape. Creatures living here were thought of as a Mist Being. Creatures had no definite form, they were to change in later times to living things as we know them. Various beings disagreed and fought among themselves, and the entire population emerged upward into the blue world. On the way up, they gathered some mountain dirt which contained the evils of the first world.

Second World-Blue World

Blue Feathered Beings inhabited this world. Also there were larger insects such as locusts and crickets. The world contained a number of chambers, and the first man and his companions traveled through the various chambers. The houses were of different shapes, and the Beings living in them were at war with one another. Everywhere the people went they saw sorrow and suffering. For this reason the Beings pleaded to leave, and into the Third World they went.

Third World-Yellow World

In this world they found squirrels, chipmunks, mice, turkeys, fox, deer, lizards and snakes. Also the Cat Spider and Grasshopper People, all who were similar in that they had no definite form.

The coyote was always curious. One day he saw the child of Water Monster. He picked up the baby and hid it under his are [sic.]

Soon afterward it began to rain, and their come [sic] a great flood. The People climbed the Mountains, but the water continued to rise. Finally, the first man planted a woman reed, which brought them to the Fourth World. Entering, the

People noticed that the coyote was hiding something. They searched him and found Water Monster's baby. They reasoned that this caused the flood. The coyote was told, the baby goes back, and he did so.

Fourth World-Glittering World

First man and first woman formed the main four sacred mountains from the soil the first man had gathered from the Third World. They found pueblos in the Fourth World. Changing Woman, in the present day world, created the four original clans.

We'd wandered into the Center to inquire about tours of the Valley. By the time I had read the display through to 'The coyote was told, the baby goes back...' I decided I had to take this elegant evolutionary summation away with me. (I beg forgiveness for any mistakes I may have made in transcription.) The Center's murky lighting system cast oblique shadows over the tall displays, and several Navajo men lurked in the corners, steeping forward to speak in clandestine tones to the tourists. I was a little worried that they might object to my theft of their creation myth, but they ignored me and continued to offer their Valley tours.

The book, Canyon de Chelly: The Story Behind the Scenery (KC Publications, Inc; 1990) states on page 43: "...the old timer *bilagaana* (white men) know that the Navajo sense of humor is manifested in colorful stories made up for the sake of gullible tourists. The Navajo sees no harm in this; he gets a good chuckle and the tourist goes away satisfied." So maybe I was providing entertainment for those men in the shadowy corners.

We decided to forgo a tour and drive the Valley on our own. The teenage girl in the entrance booth twinkled solemnly at us and said, "Okay, I'll give you an entrance ticket, but I've been told to warn you that there are wild Indians inside the Park today." She was referring to a hundred third graders on a forced march down the park road with their teachers. They straggled along, dragging their knapsacks, stopping to take short breaks in the dust and then regrouping in exhausted formations. Some of them gave our car a floppy wave as we passed. They were the brothers and sisters of the children who hung about with their parents at roadside tables selling jewelry and small pots throughout the Navajo Nation, announced by signs reading Nice Indians Up Ahead. Further down the road another sign would declare, Nice Indians Behind You.

We had wandered the dusty expanses of the Nation for weeks now, traveling for hours down rutted roads to reach ancient Indian sites, growing bored and tired and then suddenly encountering some dramatic site that would startle us back to excitement. Farmington, Shiprock, Tohatchie, Window Rock, Ganado, Chinle, Mexican Water, Kayente. All under a huge sky that entertained us with fantastic cloud drifts and far off rain showers where the clouds met the ground. Wind and more wind. Pickups with Navajo plates zipping past us on the numbered Indian Routes, leaving blooming fogs of dust to settle over us. Horses, cows, sheep, dogs and chickens wandering across the roads, beneficiaries of the open range policy of the Nation. It was a land where you kept your gas tank filled and lost track of time.

Finally, Monument Valley, our last official stop before we turned eastward. When I was ten years old I had decided I would come here someday. My younger brother and I would be lounging in the back seat of the family Chevrolet where it was parked on a upward tilt, Mom and Dad in the front seat, gray sound box clipped to the driver's window, a western playing out on the movie screen against the night sky. Inevitably my father would say, "Well, they shot that in Monument Valley." Peering through the thick humidity of southern Vermont in July, I would watch men on horseback thunder through a barren landscape of huge and strangely shaped cliffs. Dad's happy voice and the cinematic scenery merged into a determination to see the real place.

My parents both grew up in California, Dad on the wealthy side of Pasadena, and Mom on the less fortunate but still genteel side. The first year of their marriage they traveled east to tour New England, a place that my mother had dreamed of when she was a little girl. As she would tell her children, they motored up the Maine coast, and in Damariscotta she decided she was meant to live in New England. Bucking the American trend, they moved east and spent most of their married years in the demanding seasons of Maine and Vermont. Before marrying, my father had spent happy weeks of his single years camping throughout the west, when camping meant traveling on horses and hunting for fresh meat to supplement the canned goods that the packhorses had carried in. Years later, the sight of Monument Valley in a movie called forth the longing and nostalgia in his voice that had fixed this place in my mind.

One of the decaying home movies found in Mom's basement was labeled "High Sierra Camping Trip, 1932" and depicted in twenty minutes of jerky black and white footage a pack trip by five men on horseback and half a dozen pack animals. I imagine Dad balancing his chunky camera on a tripod atop a rocky outcrop in order to film a scene of horses and men on foot negotiating a rocky switchback trail. Muscles in the horses' flanks ripple and quiver; the men scramble one by one up out of camera range. Rocks knocked loose by the climbers bounce away down the steep slope. The view cuts to a barren ridge top. A man's hat appears, and one of the campers struggles to the crest. The lens watches the following line of men and horses mount the pinnacle and slide down out of sight again. The scene shifts to a woodsy setting, where a deer stands alert in a clearing. Quick cut to two men struggling with a dead buck, heaving and yanking to get the animal strung up on a tree limb. Their movements stutter like an old Laurel and Hardy movie. One of the men approaches with a knife and makes a slicing motion near the throat. The screen blackens, severing the scene, and then flickers alive again to document the campfire with a flat griddle laid over it. The cook jerks about, juggling pots. The men grin into the lens while they tear at their food with bared teeth. Subtitles name them: Doc, Bud, Chic, Dad, and Camera Man. The last one was my dad.

He punctuated the film with captions: "After an all day climb with no lunch, what could be more welcome than Come and Get It?" "Everyone has good appetites at 10,000 Feet!" "Copper Pass: Thrills aplenty at 12,00 feet!" Two hands point to a sign: "Elizabeth Pass, 11,000 feet." The last caption announces: "Home at Last: Happy and Tired!!" Around the corner of a stucco house set in manicured gardens strides a grinning man, very dirty and very skinny, carrying the horns of a buck.

This was the west that had brought forth that nostalgia in my father's voice. Now Interstates networked the nation, horses had become the playthings of the wealthy, and the middle class was more apt to scale peaks in RVs than in the saddle.

In Monument Valley we stayed at Gouldings, a resort built in the nineteen-thirties, arriving in a dust storm that covered the landscape in thick grit. We established camp on a steep hill overlooking a canyon cut and holed up inside the RV to watch the purple iris by our picnic bench whip sideways in the red dirt. Not much else was visible through the window. Murray and I ventured outside for a quick turn to oblige his needs and then retreated, eyes and throats burning. Hours inched by, the camper rocked in the wind, my companions napped, and I read and wondered why we'd come here. M awoke, and we spoke longingly of home.

To pass the time we visited the resort's museum. Photos and artifacts celebrated long dead film people, on vacation or on location to shoot a movie. The inevitable homage to John Wayne included shots of bulky gray tents with men in ten-gallon hats lined up in front of them.

My own western hero is my father, born in 1902 and a horse camper until he married at age thirty-four. He must have been in the Valley either before Gouldings was here or as one of the very early visitors. The resort's gray tents would have been a luxury for him. Now here I was in one of his favorite places, in my thirty-one-foot RV, complete with indoor kitchen and bathroom and a hard roof between the weather and me. I think he would have gotten a kick out of it.

The second day of our visit the wind subsided to reveal a spectacular view down through the mouth of our canyon and out to the mesas, buttes and spires of the Valley. We drove the rough dirt road from vista to vista, waving to those weary third graders. Fantastic shifting colors of russet, ochre, grey, black, cadmium, rose and violet decorated twisting sinuous shapes that had hardened into stone and were sometimes crumbling into dust. All against a thick blue sky, with no sign of green life except the pale beige whisk of grass here and there, biding its time for better, rainy days. The car bumped along the road, a metal insect lost among the rocky shapes. Surely when my father was here there was no turnout labeled "John Ford's Point." The road itself could have been the same one that he had traveled; there certainly hadn't been any improvements to it in decades. We rocked and slammed through ruts and crevasses at ten miles an hour while carved shapes thrust up around us and I remembered the drive-in movie in southern Vermont.

My inexhaustible sightseer of a husband said, "Okay, let's go home." We packed up and turned eastward onto Route 163, carrying with us a coat of thick, red dust. I said a silent thank you to my dad and picked up my knitting needles.

24

God Given Time

We had gone out onto the hardpan of North America in the midst of a drought season. We traveled home across a greening crust, with May flouncing its blossoms over the landscape and flood warnings on the radio signaling the end of aridity in most of the country. We had gone traveling like two kids on a lark. We'd encountered our worst marital fighting in years. The change in daily circumstances upended our established balances and opened up the consideration of fearful new issues between us. I had brooded more on my family origins than I had since my twenties. When the last parent dies, the end of one's life takes tactile shape and forces a consideration of the whole arc of one's own time. A marriage that already encompasses almost half of that time must come under examination.

Travel promised a route out of ourselves, an invitation to imagine alternate lives that we might have lived. An alien cityscape can evoke nostalgic longing for what one might have been if one spoke French instead of English, or had inherited a shoe manufacturer's fortune, or had dropped out of college and hitchhiked to Salinas before one's parents paid the tuition bill, or, conversely, had studied hard enough to earn a year at Oxford and stayed on there. Travel teases us with the embodiment of forfeited choices. Choked with vicarious grief, the traveler dangles her hand in the flowing waters of loss for a short time, pulling it out before she is swept away.

On our eastward return home we stopped in Pennsylvania to tour Frank Lloyd Wright's concoction at Fallingwater. Here cousins who had married each other in order to avoid the dissipation of family wealth played out many of their leisure hours in surroundings of great artistry and questionable engineering. A waterfall gurgles through the living room. The guide's sharp eye prevented me from wetting my hand next to the low-slung couch here. Her circumspect description of the wife's death by probable suicide brought up short my musings over the consequences if my own forbearers had been wiser about conserving the family fortune.

We went on, heading for northern Vermont and my mother's interment on a May morning thick with mosquitoes. She had possessed her own gift for self-creation. Almost thirty years old when she first saw New England, she had come to embody the Yankee characteristics of stoicism and strength on rocky soil that she so effectively taught to me. The West that my parents spoke of was their own youth. Their children grew up as Easterners.

M and I had lived for the first three years of our marriage in San Diego, before coming back to the right side of the continent. On half a dozen other occasions I had traveled to California in an airplane for short visits. So when we headed backwards across the map page in our new RV, the country between the coasts existed in my mind mostly as a sketchy outline. Covering the miles inch by inch on rolling tires, we sought depth and intimacy in the solid earth. We could have chosen to stay home for our year off, slipped out of the yoke of salaried time and spent the months exploring Boston's many secret recesses. We never considered it. The trip gave us a purpose, organized the time, demanded a commitment, laid out choices and imposed the need for decisions.

We had started out with lists of imperatives: places to see, things to do. Some of the high points of the year had been nowhere in those catalogs: Big Bend, Abiquiu, and the Hood Canal. Some of the low points too: 9/11. Mom's death. The worst of our fights.

A month after returning to Brookline we were riding home from a restaurant in the back of some friends' car, when the wife suddenly twisted around and smiled at us from between the two front seats. "You guys are different together."

"How?" We were holding hands, but we did that before we went away.

"You laugh more." More? Maybe. A bumper sticker stuck to an aging trailer in a campground in Louisiana flashed in my thoughts: Too old to work, too young to die, so here we are, just Mom and I. Too dreary.

I had headed west heedless of the real difficulties that awaited us, with vague ideas of discovering a new life and indulging in a little of the reinvention that my mother seemed so good at. There were times in those last twelve months that I'd felt way over my head. If at age fifty-seven I'd gone looking for the life I wanted to live, I was a bit late. If M felt that way, he didn't say it.

We may travel in order to arrive at the present, but I had spent an inordinate amount of time thinking about the past. I had finally accepted that all moods are transitory and uncontrollable. Happiness will give way to sadness, and again to cheer. Outward circumstances only partially influence this flow. The one chance at any mastery you can have of your emotions is to give yourself up to the cycle.

Yet this I know: The discipline and self control that I first remember consciously learning in the early homesick months at boarding school, strengthened through the long years of work, has born me well. It goes with me to whatever comes next. And glad I am of it.

And what of M and me? That night in the car, my friend remarked not on two individuals, but on a relationship. We had lived together on the road, where the challenges dealt at least as much with the daily monotony of life as they did with the new and exciting. Perhaps this involvement with the tiresome difficulties of vehicles, strange geography, moods and physical symptoms, all lived out in a space with fractional elbowroom, had been what most changed us. It would be satisfying to report that a calm and loving conversation about our mutual future had followed the fight at the Biosphere. It hadn't. Gain in a marriage can sometimes be measured by the times you turn away from an issue, use a soft remark and a change of subject in a conversation that teeters towards a flash point. You each get breathing, thinking space.

The thinking goes on. Thank God. When that's over, it's all over, and I am way not ready.

Nothing went precisely as planned when we got home. I found work twice in the following year, and twice I quickly realized I could no longer stand the sadness and frustration of social work. I quit, first after two months, then after six. My brothers started to tease me, called me their sister who couldn't keep a job. It seemed that I wasn't the only one who'd thought that I was Little Miss Responsibility.

We moved to the country. A house on a lake, where the light on the water changes colors and depths throughout the day. We had talked for years of such a place. We ticked off the achievement of another dream on the list. Learning to love country living by escaping regularly back to the city, we accepted again that nothing is static. Perhaps the years ahead will be measured by the dreams we achieve. And, of course, the grief we endure.

978-0-595-40699-9
0-595-40699-8

Printed in the United States
64827LVS00005BA/82